SIR THOMAS BEECHAM

by the same author

Autobiography
Second Innings
Cricket All the Year
Close of Play
Talking of Music

NEVILLE CARDUS

Sir Thomas Beecham

A MEMOIR

COLLINS

St James's Place, London

1961

Printed in Great Britain
Collins Clear-Type Press
London and Glasgow

TO LADY BEECHAM
AND MEMBERS OF
THE ROYAL
PHILHARMONIC
ORCHESTRA

CONTENTS

The Man 15

A Conversation Piece 69

Musician and Conductor 79

ILLUSTRATIONS

Frontispiece

With Agnes Nicholls, the wife of Sir Hamilton Harty, in 1922 *facing page* 40

At work 41

Playing the piano 96

Broadcasting 97

Listening to himself 112

At rehearsal 113

ACKNOWLEDGMENTS

My thanks are due to Messrs. Hutchinson and Company for permission to quote from Sir Thomas's books, *A Mingled Chime* and *Frederick Delius* and to Mr. Alastair Hetherington, Editor of the *Guardian*, for permission to reproduce Sir Thomas's letter to his paper. For permission to include the illustrations, my thanks are due to Mr. Evan Senior, Mr. Sydney J. Loeb, The Royal Opera House, Covent Garden, the Keystone Press and Mr. Erich Auerbach.

London, 1961 NEVILLE CARDUS

The Man

MY FIRST MEETING WITH SIR THOMAS BEECHAM was at the Salzburg Festival in 1931. Correspondence had taken place between us before this eventful year in my life. In 1929 Sir Thomas conducted all the major music of Delius in the Queen's Hall; he persuaded the blind and paralysed composer to travel from his home at Grez-sur-Loing to London. Sir Thomas chanced to come upon an article I had written about Delius in the "Manchester Guardian"—as this newspaper was then very rightly called. He wrote me a short note which pleased me immensely: "I have read your piece on Frederic Delius with much interest. It should be preserved. Yours, Thomas Beecham." "Preserved!" He could pick out a word and give it a new relish. "Preserved!"—in the context of his letter I have rolled the word over on my palate for thirty and more years. It still retains its first flavour.

At Salzburg in 1931 I was astounded one day in the Festival's second week to get a telephone message from Sir Thomas asking me to lunch with him at the Europa Hotel. He had gone to the trouble to find out that I was staying at the Stein Hotel. He was engaged to conduct at the Salzburg Festival that year. I didn't dream he would wish to know me personally, so with some trepidation I went to the Europa. Rain was falling in thick curtains—*Schnürlregen*. Sir Thomas came down from his room after the reception office had rung him. He came down not by the lift but by the stairs. As he descended them they assumed, in imagination's eye, red carpet. There were many distinguished people present in the Europa's foyer; but all eyes turned on Sir Thomas, whether he was a familiar or unfamiliar sight to those looking. The image of Sir Thomas to-day in the memory of our nation is of a G.O.M., moving in state, slowly and portly, almost benignly institutional. In the prime of his life he stood upright without stiffness, the easy charm of Oxford mingling with the confident alertness of a Commander-in-Chief sniffing the battle. He dressed in the best Savile Row stuffs and cut—in the daytime usually wearing a grey double-breasted coat. He could wear new clothes in a way which made them appear weeks old on their first outing. His blue eyes took in at one swift scrutiny a whole scene in the Europa foyer, and at once he picked me out of the human traffic. He took me by the shoulder, leading me to the elegant cocktail bar. When he asked me to choose an "Aperitif," I suggested sherry. To tell the truth I was not at this time of my career greatly experienced in cocktails or wine, or in hotels called "Europa" and the like. "No, my dear fellow, not sherry," said Sir Thomas, "very liverish, sherry—for a musical critic. Consider Ernest Newman. Try a 'White Lady.'"

In 1959 I dined alone with Sir Thomas in London in Brown's Hotel. He had just lost Lady Betty. As soon as I entered his suite, he called the waiter. "Bring Mr. Neville Cardus a 'White Lady.'" Then, turning to me he added, " I bought you your first ' White Lady ' at Salzburg, didn't I? " In his crowded never-resting life he had remembered a remote detail as insignificant as this, at a time of mourning and loss, and nearing his eightieth year.

After our ' White Ladies ' that wet day at Salzburg, we went into the dining-room. To my unease and, at the moment, my disappointment, we were joined by Lady Cunard, bird-like canary and voluble. Sir Thomas introduced me—" of the ' Manchester Guardian'."

" Ah," quick-fired Lady Cunard, " ah, now, Mr. Cardus —you must write an article—protesting against this English obsession about foreign music—we can do just as well in England—so please, write at once a strong article in the ' Liverpool Post.' " " ' Manchester Guardian,' " prompted Sir Thomas.

" Ah, yes," prattled Lady Cunard, " you know it is simply absurd—the adulation in England of all that is foreign—really, Mr. Cardus—please write a very strong article in the ' Yorkshire Post.' " " ' Manchester Guardian,' " insisted Sir Thomas, chewing his short Imperial beard.

" Ah, yes," persisted Lady Cunard, taking new breath, " it is too ridiculous—this blind worship of everything foreign in music—you simply must, Mr. Cardus, make a strong protest in——"

" The ' Manchester Guardian,' " prompted Sir Thomas yet again, this time his voice a little weary. I found myself in a new world of comedy and play, in which conversation was a game between lively minds delighting in a scene, a " situation," to be savoured histrionically; life set continuously on a stage brilliant and well-bred. No wonder Sir Thomas and Lady Cunard found most plays presented in a London theatre not a little dim, dowdy and under-acted. Sir Thomas's entire waking days and years were presented to an audience; I often wondered what manner of man he was when alone and unobserved.

Lady Cunard was a patron of music in the halcyon period, before the advent of an Arts Council. I met her only once again after our fortuitous coming together at Salzburg. Through the Mephistophelian agency of Sir Thomas I went one Sunday to lunch at Lady Cunard's in Grosvenor Square. Many distinguished people were present. Towards late afternoon, as we all sat in the drawing-room, Lady Cunard curdled my blood by asking me to play the piano. The world in general takes for granted the ability of a music-critic to play the piano—not the horn, trombone or tuba. As I have never commanded the rudiments of a pianist, I declined Lady Cunard's invitation to take a seat at her Bechstein. " Oh, please do," reiterated Lady Cunard, and her request was echoed throughout the salon, in various accents. " Plis," " Bitte," with encouraging smiling faces thrust forward at me. " But, really," I implored, " really, Lady Cunard, I can't—I am not even a tinkler of a pianist." Then Sir Thomas spoke: " It is just like him " (imagine the drawl and the mischievous glint in his eyes), " he is as a matter of fact, a very fine player. His Chopin is remarkable, comparable in felicity of touch with Pachman's."

Sir Thomas had never seen me sitting anywhere near

a keyboard. I again assured Lady Cunard that I could not and would not play. None the less, everybody apparently took Sir Thomas's word for gospel truth. In this way I achieved amongst a select and distinguished circle of high society in London a reputation to which I was not born and had never achieved by performance, a reputation thrust on me. Seldom did Sir Thomas resist an opportunity to turn a situation into sardonic comedy. It was on this occasion at Lady Cunard's that he came out with one of his most famous sayings. He rose suddenly from his chair, excusing himself for an early departure. "I have to see my solicitor to discuss matters in which the Official Receiver is interested and, on my behalf, very much concerned. And for what he is about to receive, may the Lord make him truly thankful." He timed his remark so perfectly that the last word "thankful" was uttered as he closed the door of the drawing-room behind him.

He was a comedian. Or, as this is a term which the English associate with red-nosed buffoonery, I had better describe him as an artist in comedy. But he was not a wit in the epigrammatic way of Oscar Wilde, with whose sayings Beecham's are often compared. Sir Thomas indulged not so much in wit as in waggery; he was not 18th century of manner in the least. He belonged entirely to the 19th century, when wit became broadened with nature into waggery, and when the aristocrat became more closely related to an English bourgeois geniality. For all his poise of behaviour, his deliberately fastidious voice and vocabulary, he remained at bottom a Lancastrian who first saw the light of life at St. Helens. The suave accent, his button boots—(in those days)—his measured diction, didn't put those of us who knew him well off the scent. With Sir Thomas blood was thicker than water, or the sparkling and popping of Pol Roger. Away from the concert platform he never hurried, not even while crossing a busy street. One morning, after a rehearsal of the " Messiah " in the Queen's Hall a day or two before Christmas, we were about to go into the Langham Hotel for lunch. I produced from my pocket a new Dunhill pipe and said, " I know it is impossible to give any sort of Christmas present to you, Sir Thomas. But here you are—and, please try not to forget all about this one." He took the pipe, thanked me and, with a split-second of hesitation, sang to a Handelian cadence, " It shall be smoke-ed."

Where did he come from—a Lancashire family enriched by the manufacture of pills? His father, I am told, spoke uninhibited Lancashire speech. But though, as I say, some Lancastrian gusto, even some hint of provincial arrogance, could often be flavoured in his interior, breaking out in moments that found him off guard of his poise—a poise made second nature by long conscious practice—Sir Thomas's image to the public had no suspicion of regional characteristics. On the contrary, he exhibited himself as the entirely sophisticated man of the world. Only twice in all the happy hours I enjoyed his company did he talk to me of his boyhood and Beecham's Pills.

"My father," he narrated, "had an ear for music. As a present to me, when I was in my late teens, he bought an electrical organ, one of the first invented. It was built into our house just outside St. Helens. When I played on it, on a dark December night, all the lights of St. Helens were extinguished." This glimpse into his home-life was the only one he gave me in a long and intimate friendship with him. Then the pills—"My father," he confided, "came to me one Christmas and said, 'Look here, my lad, I've been spendin' a lot o' brass on your musical education, and now Ah wants you to help me.'" (Every year a Christmas Carol Annual was published by Beecham's Pills.) "'Now, Tom,' continued my father, 'I want you to go through th' Annual and alter some of th' verses so as to advertise th' business, you know.'" "So," Sir Thomas told me, "I retired into my study and, after some meditation, I produced the following:

> Hark! the herald angels sing!
> Beecham's Pills are just the thing,
> Two for a woman one for a child . . .
> Peace on Earth and mercy mild!

"These sentiments," continued Sir Thomas, "especially the ellipsis, seemed to me admirably to express the rapture which is occasioned by a good effortless release . . ."

At times I suspected that he erected a façade to hide from the world an uncertain Beecham, a Beecham afflicted with a feeling of inferiority, of some frustration in himself. He would admit no shortcoming in his mental and musical equipment. I never heard him express disappointment with his own share in a concert or opera performance. Occasionally his conducting was as slapdash as well could be; to such a level of unconscious bluff on the rostrum could he descend that often I have blushed for him. The finale of the Seventh Symphony of Beethoven acted on him as a red rag to a bull. Several times I chastised him in print and by word of mouth after he had roared and rattled the orchestra through a composition. Invariably he would reply: " Like most of your fraternity you are from time to time visited by tone deafness. The performance in question was one of my very finest . . . You might like to know that only this morning So-and-So rang me up to tell me he had never heard a better . . ." So-and-So might be anybody from Strauss to his first trombone.

He housed no daemon that preyed and devoured his creative or, rather his re-creative, tissue of nerves, sensibility and power of musical thinking. He was not the haunted, tormented artist, ever deploring that his reach went far beyond his grasp. He was, in a word, vain—in two words, intractably vain. He would go into a fury at any depreciation of his activities, on or off the platform, mental or physical. He showed me one evening a photo of an old school group: the Rossall Cricket XI. " That is myself," he said, pointing to a slim youth on the back row, elegant, if beardless, in flannels. " Heavens! " I ejaculated involuntarily, " did you really play cricket? " " And why *shouldn't* I have played cricket? "—in a querulous tone, with a twitch of nose and flash of eye. " Well," I stammered

. . . "Well . . ." "I was quite a good fast bowler," he asserted, "far above the average. But I gave up cricket because at the time I intended to become a great concert pianist . . . and I could not risk my fingers in a mere game." Can we, with the wildest and most roving eye of imagination, see Sir Thomas bowling fast, probably too fast?

He was not particularly interested in outdoor sports; only once did I see him on a cricket ground. At this time he was living in Circus Road, a stone's throw from Lord's. On a sunny day, round about 1958, the M.C.C. defeated Oxford University before lunch at half past one. I didn't wish to return to the West End in glorious weather, so I wandered round Lord's for half an hour or so. Then, outside the Tavern, I saw Sir Thomas sitting on a gimcrack chair. He wore a faded panama hat and white "ducks." He was an apparition. The ground had emptied; only a few people loitered near the Tavern. "Good God!" I exclaimed, "what has brought you to Lord's?" "I thought I'd like to see my old University. And why don't they play?" I told him that the match was over and done with. "How extraordinary—just like the English," he said; "on a fine day, an extremely unlikely happening in any summer here in this country, and they don't play cricket." After a pause he added, "I had a suspicion that something was wrong. They admitted me into the ground without payment."

Where and how did I propose to spend the remainder of the afternoon, he asked, as we walked out of Lord's.

" I am free until six o'clock or so," I informed him. He hailed a taxi, saying to the driver, " Take us round the more salubrious parts of North-West London." And for two hours and more the driver obeyed Sir Thomas's instructions. Mention of this taxi episode with Sir Thomas gives me a chance to knock on the head the old tale to the effect that Sir Thomas, walking down Regent Street on a hot day, took off his overcoat, called a taxi, flung the overcoat into it, and continued his walk, saying to the driver, " Follow me." This story is untrue, both to fact and to character. Several stories about Sir Thomas, though not true in fact, are true to character. One or two (at least) I invented and put into circulation myself—no, I didn't invent, but gave a twist to a Beecham saying for which, on the spur of the inspired moment, he could not quite find the only clinching phrase. Long after his seventieth birthday, we argued one evening for an hour, trying to establish once and for all the authenticity and origin of certain Beecham quips. He accused me of making-up and foisting on him, a question supposedly put by him to a singer in his opera company. This singer was a splendid actor of parts such as Klingsor and Alberich. He asked Sir Thomas for advice—" About my son—he'll be leaving Oxford next year. I've spent a lot of money on him and he doesn't know what sort of a job to take up." Beecham stroked his chin.

" Aren't you going to make a singer of him ? "

" Oh, no, Sir Thomas."

" But, why ? "

" Well—he hasn't got a voice, not really."

" Ah," said Sir Thomas, in dulcet tones, " ah, I see—a family failing."

Sir Thomas persisted that the crack was mine, that he hadn't said and couldn't say, anything so cruel. I reduced him to silence, as far as this argument was concerned, by assuring him that nobody else, living in England since Oscar Wilde, could spontaneously have produced wit as swift to the target as this. Vanity in him could be exalted to pride on stilts. At Salzburg, during the same Festival at which I first met him, he emphasised Lady Cunard's tirade against the preference in England for foreign as against English music and musicians. " I could produce opera to-morrow just as good as they produce it here, or anywhere else." " Maybe," I replied, " *You* could produce opera in England, no doubt. But here, in Salzburg, if all the singers, instrumentalists, musicians, technicians and Bruno Walter were somehow killed in a train or plane accident or got drowned in the rain and the overflowing river Salzach, the Salzburg Festival would still go on—they'd bring a fresh opera company over from Munich or Vienna . . ."

" Well," sniffed Sir Thomas, " what of it? "

" Why," I said, " if you were giving a Festival in England and only *you*—you alone—chanced to die suddenly, the Festival would collapse inevitably, irreparably . . ."

" Nons——" shouted Sir Thomas, then pulled himself together, just in time. " You are quite right—quite right." He simply could not say " Nonsense." I had drawn *him* along the garden path. But his vanity didn't irritate, he couldn't help it. He was born that way. And to vary the saying of another great Englishman, he had quite a lot to be vain about.

In all the countless hours I spent with him, nobody else present, I never heard him refer to religion. To women he referred to once, saying that none was worth the loss of a night's sleep. His reading was extensive rather than wide. He did nothing to correct or modify personal prejudice. He was allergic to anything German. "How can you read Goethe?" he would ask, "he was a colossal and conceited bore, and something of a dabbler." (He, by the way, knew little German.) Heine, of course, appealed to him, good translation or bad. "He was a Jew, therefore not even the German language could get in the way of his wit." Whenever I drew his attention to Goethe's love poems he would really let himself go. "A literary affectation. Goethe ran away from sex; he was a spinster." German music he pretended to belittle; but at the bottom of his heart, he respected it. Bach was one of his pet aversions. "Too much counterpoint—moreover, Protestant counterpoint." "And Wagner . . .?" "A genius, no doubt; but too often excessively theatrical and emotional. 'Lohengrin' was his only stylish work—the Germans have no idea of style." "But what about 'Meistersinger'?" The fugue in the overture, he said, was the crudest example of that always dreary form of music, the crudest example in existence. On the whole he admitted the broad humanity of " Meistersinger," adding that whenever he conducted this opera he needed for the time being to forget Mozart's " Figaro " and " Falstaff " of Verdi. He delighted in French lyric opera. " I would give the whole of Bach's Brandenburg concertos for Massenet's ' Manon ' and would think I had vastly profited by the exchange. Bach composed in only two tempi—quick and slow. Bach's music is associated in Protestant countries with Biblical texts, which are sacrosanct." " But," I protested, " Stainer composed to a religious text, and nobody allowed sacrosanct words and associations to deafen them to poor music." " Stainer, my dear fellow, doesn't come into our argument, which, I take it, is concerned with music and musicians. Nearly all the questionable works of the great musical geniuses have been prompted by religion, or by implications of religion. For instance, Wagner's ' Parsifal,' the ' Requiem ' of Brahms, and Elgar's ' Gerontius,' described by my friend George Moore as holy water in a German beer barrel . . . Dvorak's ' Stabat Mater,' Gounod's ' Redemption '—can you believe that quite a number of civilised musicians could listen to such stuff? What dreadful crimes have been committed in the name of religion! Gounod normally was a sensitive artist, and Dvorak composed an enchanting symphony—the Fourth. The ' Missa Solemnis ' is mostly second-rate Beethoven, or rather, it is third-rate Beethoven. The best of Beethoven's music, excepting the first four of his piano concertos, and the third, fourth and sixth of his symphonies, is second rate, measured by values set up by Mozart . . . Vaughan Williams? I very much like his ' Fantasia on a Theme of Tallis.' Unfortunately, in his compositions published subsequently to the 'Fantasia on a Theme of Tallis' he omitted to take the precaution of including a theme by Tallis."

So he would go on outrageously, sometimes foolishly, yet the humour twinkled so much in his eyes and in the twitching of nose and beard that all acerbity was thawed. Often there was a grain of sense in his chaff. His judgment of a Bruckner symphony, facetious on the surface though it might seem, went straight to the point of Bruckner's occasional inability to develop and organise a movement. "In the first movement I took note of a dozen pregnancies—and half a dozen miscarriages." But he actually chose the Seventh Symphony of Bruckner for a performance in the Third programme of the B.B.C. In fact, he chose it for two performances on successive evenings, played by the B.B.C. orchestra. But the second performance was conducted not by Sir Thomas but by Mr. Paul Beard. I spoke to Sir Thomas next day over the telephone. "Were you ill last night, Sir Thomas?—I hope not." "Why should you think that I was?" "Well, you didn't conduct the second broadcast of the Bruckner Seventh." "No, my dear fellow, I didn't and couldn't. One performance was quite enough, as far as I was concerned." "But why did you choose to conduct a Bruckner symphony at all? You know that you find him perpetually tedious." "My dear fellow," came the famous drawl over the telephone, "my orchestra lately has been complaining of lack of work. I've been away on the Continent. So I decided that they should play a work which would keep them fully occupied for quite a time."

He took delight in maltreating a composition he didn't like. On one occasion he found himself obliged to conduct the " Pastoral " symphony of Vaughan Williams. Moreover he was audacious enough to rehearse the symphony without score. He just " followed " the players. The symphony ends with an orchestral descent to near silence, then a soprano sings the final cadence. Sir Thomas, after waiting until the voice died away, waiting with a superb show of impatience, turned to the first violins and made an imperious down-beat. No instrumentalist, of course, produced a sound. " Why don't you play? " asked Sir Thomas. Quite a number of people were present at this rehearsal, so the first violin, wishing to save Sir Thomas's face, whispered, " There's nothing else to play, Sir Thomas." " Nothing else to play? " queried Sir Thomas in a loud unashamed voice, audible throughout the hall—" thank God! "

He could not be " put down "; in this respect he was Falstaffian. He was amoral in argument; his wit insisted on asserting itself. Round about the 1930s he astonished me by telling me that he proposed to present Alan Berg's " Wozzeck " at Covent Garden, which was then under his direction. " I shall go into the country and study the score." Three or four weeks later I received an invitation from him to lunch at Abbey Lodge, his address (of many addresses) at this time. When the valet led me to Sir Thomas's room the strains of " One fine day " from

"Madame Butterfly" floated on the air, played on the piano. And as I went into his room Sir Thomas was at the piano. "Why Puccini?" I asked. "I am trying to wash 'Wozzeck' from my mind and memory." He did not "present" the music-drama at Covent Garden, needless to say. "It is an ingenious score," he admitted, "but entirely uncivilised and uncharming. I am not interested in music, or in any work of art, that fails to stimulate enjoyment in life, and, what is more, pride in life." He was not really a narrow-minded reactionary. Sir Thomas, when he was fairly young in years, introduced London, and nearly all the important cities of England, to music which was at the time called "modern"—Stravinsky, Delius, Debussy, Ravel and the Russians. He even conducted the A flat symphony of Elgar, which, by the way, was played a hundred times in this country in the year of its first performance at a Hallé Concert, under Hans Richter. Beecham severely "cut" the work and Elgar protested. At Sir Thomas's next rehearsal of the symphony he addressed the orchestra thus: "Gentlemen, the composer of this immortal masterpiece objects to my abbreviations. So now we'll play it as written—with all the repeats." The point of this ironic arrow will be felt by musicians who know that the A flat symphony is governed by a recurrent "motto-theme" and a cyclic development. "Elgar's A flat symphony," he informed me, "is a large work." "But," I retorted, "there are many 'large' works." "Maybe," he said, "but this is a particularly large work." He none the less conducted

Elgar's "Enigma" variations to perfection, which is proof that he could respond sympathetically to a work if its style and *Stimmung* were not alien to his very personal æsthetics of music, no matter how much he might dislike the composer's output as a whole. His preferences occasionally baffled even those of his friends who imagined that they were aware of his eccentricities. He was attracted to the vital personality of Ethel Smyth, that very great Englishwoman who, though her music is to-day forgotten, persuaded many of Germany's finest conductors to accept her as the first of all really important women composers. Her operas were produced in many a German centre of musical culture. If I am remembering rightly, her opera "The Wreckers" was conducted at Covent Garden by Bruno Walter. Sir Thomas thought highly of "The Wreckers." "The vigour and rhythmic force of parts of this opera equals anything of the kind written in my time." He conducted an oratorio by Ethel Smyth called "The Prison," and by his own transforming genius made the music eloquent and so convincing that I persuaded the Hallé Concerts Society to perform it in Manchester. At a second hearing the performance, not conducted by Sir Thomas, the truth was revealed—the music was merely good well-remembered stuff, which now burned like a black slow fire.

He accepted an invitation in 1928 to conduct the New York Philharmonic. This magnificent orchestra was then in charge of Toscanini; and the Maestro at the time was far away in Italy. Beecham was called in as a temporary substitute. After his first rehearsal with the New York players, he was taken to lunch by the orchestra's committee —large opulent men crinkling with dollar notes, and aromatic with enormous cigars. They asked Sir Thomas to give his opinion of the Philharmonic. "They are quite incredibly good," he said, flavouring his Havana; "their technical command is abnormal . . . I have rehearsed Rimsky-Korsakov's 'Schéhérazade' this morning. The woodwinds and horns executed the most difficult arabesques like Kreisler on his violin. Really wonderful." Now the menacing pause. "But for all this dexterity of technique, I found the players extraordinarily insensitive interpretatively. No idea of an alluring phrase . . ." Another pause, then —"Tell me, who has been conducting your orchestra lately?"

It was during this visit to New York, so Sir Thomas asked me to believe, that, as he lay in bed one night, the telephone rang. "Who is it?" he asked. "Is thart Sir Tammas Beech'm?" "It is." "Well, A'm the seketry of the English Speak'n Oonion of Noo York." "I beg your pardon?"—"Are you Sir Tammas Beech'm?" "Yes, I am." "Well, Ah'm tellin' you, Ah'm the seketry of the English Speakin' Oonion of Noo York . . ." "I don't believe it. Good night." And Sir Thomas replaced the receiver.

Like many men sharp of tongue he, as I have already suggested, was extremely sensitive to criticism of himself.

He withdrew my Press tickets for the whole of a Covent Garden season because I had taken him to task for putting on "Der Rosenkavalier" with unintelligent cuts. In drawing attention, in the "Manchester Guardian," to Sir Thomas's scissoring of "Der Rosenkavalier" I was fully aware that the opera is often produced with excisions. My point was that Sir Thomas's "cuts" in Act I were not fair to the Baron Ochs, and that because of them the audience would be left wondering why the Marschallin so heartily despised him in her outburst "*Da geht er hin*". Sir Thomas picked up his pen and rushed into print, defending himself by attack. He wrote a letter, not to my paper but to the "Daily Telegraph." His point was that in the second week of December 1912—(the performance occasioning my criticism was, circa, 1934)—he went to Berlin and discussed the production of "Der Rosenkavalier" with Strauss and Fürstner, Strauss's publisher. "On no occasion," wrote Sir Thomas, "was the suggestion ever made that the work should be given in its entirety . . . Now, as I understand him, Mr. Neville Cardus is suggesting that the man who has occupied for more than thirty years a position of pre-eminent authority in European music, and who at any moment could have insisted upon conditions anywhere respecting the production of any of his works,is to be pitied as a powerless and protesting cipher, deeply wronged by the world of music." But I had written to Strauss in Garmisch about the matter and he assured me that he had not consented to the "cuts," adding that he had "to put up with them so long as the inviolability of works of art were not protected by law." He wrote to me with considerable heat.

For weeks Sir Thomas would not see me. I called at his flat, then in Hallam Street, behind the Queen's Hall. His valet Smith informed me that Sir Thomas's instructions were that he wasn't at home to Mr. Cardus, and that, if possible, he, Smith, should throw me carefully into the area. The operative words of this instruction are "if possible." Sir Thomas and I laughed the fracas out of memory, over a lunch. And I sent him an edition de luxe of one of my cricket books, inscribed:

To Sir Thomas
from One Authority on Cuts
to Another

Like most of his colleagues, he was seldom impressed favourably by any exponent of the mysterious art of conducting excepting himself. After a slapdash concert on the pier at Bournemouth, when he seemed determined to drive the fifth symphony of Beethoven into the sea, there to be drowned beyond all hope that the body would ever be recovered, he entertained a number of friends in his suite. (If he were staying only for a night he would insist on a suite.) When we sat down at the table, the time of night was eleven o'clock. To my horror, and the horror was possibly shared by the other guests, he had chosen as part of the repast, *Homard à l'Américaine* ; and from his place at the top of the table (he was in his dressing-gown and pyjamas) he addressed—yes *addressed*—

me. "I have chosen *Homard à l'Américaine* especially for you, because I seem to remember that Grant Richards in his biography, says that *Homard à l'Américaine* is one of your favourite dishes." Grant Richards, the publisher of my first book, relates in his "Author Hunting" that when he entertained me to lunch at the Midland Hotel, Manchester, he ordered "*Homard à l'Américaine*," a delicacy which in 1922 I had never before heard of. I had forgotten the occasion myself on this festive Beecham occasion at a Bournemouth hotel in 1935, or thereabouts. Beecham's memory again!

During this midnight repast the conversation got on the subject of conductors.

"Toscanini?" asked Sir Thomas, "what do I think of Toscanini? A glorified Italian bandmaster! Have you ever heard the lively band competitions in Paris? Toscanini would have found his métier there . . . Much is made of the fact that he always conducts without a score. There is, by the way, at least one other conductor who doesn't use a score. But Toscanini is so short-sighted that he wouldn't be able to use a score . . . But though it is generally known that Toscanini invariably conducts from memory, and though it is generally known that he is half-blind, nobody apparently is aware that also he is stone deaf. Hence his performances—waiter, bring another bottle of Bollinger." A pretty girl nervously put forward the name of Bruno Walter.

"Bruno Walter? Malodorous, my dear. As for Koussevitzky, I doubt if he can read a score at all. Richter was a mere time beater. I admit that I was very young when I heard him but my earliest impressions of his conducting were confirmed by Cosima Wagner. Weingartner no doubt had a very fine musical culture. But he became slower and slower. We possess conductors of our own who are the equals of, not to say the superiors of, any of these foreigners." (In later years he asked why we in England engaged at our concerts so many third-rate Continental conductors, since we had so many second-raters of our own.) He had a good word to say of Furtwängler, whom he invited to conduct " Tristan und Isolde " at Covent Garden. But when I stated, in my notice of the performance, that Furtwängler's interpretation of the opera was the best heard in London in many long years, Sir Thomas withdrew my tickets again. Himself he had conducted " Tristan " at the Garden.

Persiflage, no doubt, but he really disliked Toscanini's conducting in the Maestro's last period. He never heard Mahler. " It is not known in this country that the most accomplished conductor since Nikisch was Richard Strauss —when he was in the right mood. His 'Tristan' was wonderful—intense but perfectly shaped. Out of mood he could be quite boring; he just wasn't interested."

Years later, in 1948, in the summer of my return to London, after seven years in Australia, Sir Thomas asked if I had heard the Hallé Orchestra lately, and what did I think of it. " Excellent," I told him. " Yes," he said, in his most dangerously alluring voice, " Yes, indeed. You know, my dear fellow, Barbirolli has done splendid work with the Hallé since they brought him back from New York. You and I have known the Hallé these many years—a good strong North of England orchestra, masculine and vigorous, first-rate in Brahms and Beethoven. Yes . . . Barbirolli has worked wonders with the Hallé. He has transformed it into the finest chamber orchestra in the country." I came soon to realise that whenever Sir Thomas lavished praise on a conductor he was up to mischief—drawing his listener down his garden's path.

I often found a difficulty distinguishing between Beecham the virtuoso conversationalist and Beecham truly expressing himself. To my bewilderment he one day contradicted a well-known English musician regarding Handel. After the well-known musician had left us, I temerariously challenged Sir Thomas: "Everything he said agreed with everything I have heard YOU say about Handel." "Maybe," sniffed Sir Thomas, "but did you expect me to agree with a nit-wit like that old bore?" To describe Sir Thomas occasionally as untruthful would be crude. He took his conversational cue from the scene, from the people to whom he was talking—like a great actor following a "script." When he told me that Puccini had assured him that only he, Sir Thomas—and not Toscanini—conducted "La Bohème" entirely to his, Puccini's, satisfaction, he somehow believed it all for the time being. (Besides, every composer dishes out the same sort of praise to whichever conductor is presenting his music to the public.)

He again drew me up his garden's path when we were talking of Benjamin Britten.

"What do you think of his 'Rape of Lucrece'?" he asked. I admired it very much, I told him. "Yes," and his eyes turned inward, "he uses a twelve-piece orchestra in 'The Rape,' doesn't he?" A pause and then, "When I was a young bachelor in London, I would sometimes wander in the purlieus of the Tottenham Court Road on summer evenings, inspecting the windows of the furniture shops, hoping to get some insight into the way the poor live. And I would see cardboard signs advertising a six-piece, or a twelve-piece suite, at such and such a price, all obtainable on the hire system. And to-day, God help us, we have lived to hear an opera with a twelve-piece orchestra—obtainable on the hire system of an Arts' Council!" Still he admitted, under cross-examination, that Britten had talent—"the only English composer worth while that has emanated from one of our colleges of music."

When the occasion suited his fancy, he attacked British musicians and British musical institutions, comparing them unfavourably with those on the Continent. But also when it suited him, he attacked Continental musicians and Continental institutions, asserting that ours were as good, if not better. Well could he have said, at any time of his life, "The brain of this foolish-compounded clay, man, is not able to invent anything that intends to laughter, more than I invent . . . I am not only witty in myself, but the cause that wit is in other men."

He sweetened a sometimes lacerating tongue with his

with Agnes Nicholls, the wife of Sir Hamilton Harty, in 1922

at work

essential genial juice. He loved life while often affecting to despise it. He was not a snob, and he was resourceful and opportunist with his charm. When he appeared one Saturday morning at a children's concert of Sir Robert Mayer, in his seventy-fifth (or thereabouts) year, he walked slowly and heavily to the rostrum, and arrived there, bowed to an audience consisting of little boys and girls, most of them not yet in their teens. He bowed to them saying, "Ladies and Gentlemen." A lovable touch. He then continued—"You must not think that my almost imperceptible progress to this rostrum was due to any reluctance on my part to conduct to an audience of children. No; my slow progress was due entirely to the infirmities of old age." Next to me, in the Royal Festival Hall, were two adorable cherubs who nearly laughed themselves out of their seats. "The first piece in our programme," continued Sir Thomas, "is by Mozart. He composed it at the age of"—he stopped short, then pointed straight at a small boy in the front row—"when he was about your age!" Master in the art of life and manners!

On the other hand, he was capable of a rudeness which a stranger to him might well and with justification call ill-bred. He roared at and insulted servants and waiters in hotels. The bark was worse than the bite; he would quickly recover composure and lavish a generous tip. Towards the end of his life he employed a handy-man to look after him. Lady Betty had recently died, and not yet had he married again. I asked him how long this handy-man had been in his service. "He was once my chauffeur.

Then he joined the army at the outbreak of the 1914 war. You will have noted that he is afflicted with a stammer. He got it this way—one morning in France he was engaged in conversation with his commanding officer. A shell from the Germans exploded between them. The commanding officer went up and up, and was never seen again . . . My chauffeur came down and down, with no greater disability than the slight stammer to which we have just referred."

Until he approached that venerable period of life during which the British people take even an artist into their bosoms unquestionably and unconditionally, he was not exactly a popular figure. " Why doesn't he pay his income tax ? " the British people asked, not knowing the complications of his financial position. " Why doesn't he live with Lady Beecham ? "—(his first wife). At about this time he walked to the conductor's desk at a concert in Birmingham in complete silence. He bowed to the audience. Not a handclap, not a sound. Whereupon he turned to the orchestra. " Let us pray," he said.

Sir Thomas has told us, in his autobiography " A Mingled Chime," how he came by the reputation of being bankrupt. I cannot here go into the complexity of it all; in fact I could not. I don't know the difference between a vendor and a residuary contract. I only know that for three or four years, dating from 1920, Sir Thomas was lost to music while he gave the whole of his time to a clearing up of the muddle of the Covent Garden Estate. His father had been persuaded to buy up this Estate with the idea of floating a public company. Then the war broke out in 1914, and the Treasury disallowed further issues of capital, other than for the resources of war. James White, better known as Jimmy White, a Lancashire man, was the first of the commercially filibustering tycoons who to-day seem likely to form a Fourth and powerful Estate. Eventually he made a fatal mistake, was brought to trial and, having been found guilty, he committed suicide. He operated from a suite in the Grand Hotel in London. One morning Sir Thomas sat in White's outer office while a barber trimmed his beard. Two Lancashire business men entered demanding an immediate interview with White. "I am afraid he is engaged at the moment," said Sir Thomas. "But we've simply *got* to see 'im," remonstrated these two men from Rochdale, "we've a lot o' brass at stake." "How much?" asked Sir Thomas. "A bloody lot, and we won't go away till we've seen him." "But," again Sir Thomas asked, "how much?" "It's a matter of £14,000." Sir Thomas then called out, "Jimmy!" And from the hinterland of the suite "Jimmy's" voice was heard, "What is it?" "A matter of petty cash," shouted Sir Thomas in reply.

In time Sir Thomas emerged from this financial labyrinth more or less successfully. Like his old friend Ernest Newman, he had an acute and well-informed brain for figures. None the less he gave his accountant, the cleverest in London, many a headache. This accountant took home with him all the papers and statistics dealing with the Covent Garden Estate and, sustained by black coffee, worked on them all night. Next morning he spoke to Sir Thomas over the telephone. " Sir Thomas," he said, " I've been going into your affairs until the crack of dawn, and now I'd like you to enlighten me on a most crucial point—do you owe, or are you owed, two million pounds? " " The answer is in the affirmative," replied Sir Thomas, " in both cases." The case went into Chancery, where the fact emerged that Sir Thomas had spent a large, not to say a vast part of his private income on music, " And what was the good of that? " asked the judge.

Sir Thomas, it is fairly well known, made his first appearance in public with the Hallé Orchestra in 1899. He was then twenty years old. His father was mayor of St. Helens, and a music lover. To give a fillip to the orchestral concerts organised and conducted by his son he decided to invite the Hallé to play in St. Helens, with Richter in charge. But Richter was unable to be present, so the young Beecham took his place, not without some technical and interpretative success. In 1912, on March 7th, Beecham (not yet, of course, Sir Thomas) conducted a Hallé Concert in Manchester. Richter had departed from Manchester in March 1911, and music in Manchester was still mainly of German origin. Beecham included in his programme Delius's " Dance Rhapsody " and Gretry's " Air for Strings." So began a long historic association with Sir

Thomas and the Hallé Concerts Society, an association to extend until 1945 and come to an end in circumstances diverting and gloriously Beechamesque. He had been appointed president of the society in 1934. During the Hitler war, the Hallé Orchestra nearly foundered; the Free Trade Hall, the orchestra's home, was bombed and partially destroyed. The critical hour called forth the man —Philip Godlee, who, as much as anybody, rescued and restored the Hallé Orchestra in the nick of time. A first salvaging move was to invite the Lord Mayor of Manchester to become president—a move calculated to open the city's purses, to the society's profit, in a time of desperate need. Sir Thomas was out of England, giving concerts in America and Australia. Apparently a letter from Godlee went astray intended to inform Sir Thomas of the reasons why the society " were making advances to the Lord Mayor of Manchester, asking that he and his successors in office should accept the position of president . . ." The details of this imbroglio are vivaciously enumerated in Michael Kennedy's classic " The Hallé Tradition." It is sufficient for my present purpose—which is to make a portrait of Sir Thomas " in the round "—to quote from the letter composed by him and sent to the " Manchester Guardian " on his return to England in 1945:

" I desire to affirm, and with all emphasis in my power, that not only am I still the President of the Hallé Society but that I have not the smallest intention of resigning or permitting myself to be removed from that position. I have also taken the step of causing to be printed on my visiting cards and business note-paper the premonitory inscription 'President of the Hallé Concerts Society.' " (" Premonitory inscription "—enchanting!)

The letter continued thus:

" I am nevertheless willing to believe that the committee " (of the Hallé Society) " may endeavour to persuade members to adopt a view of the situation other than mine. It may succeed even in getting a new president appointed; but that will not budge me from my stand. It will only mean that the society will enjoy the uncommon advantage of two presidents instead of one. Although this duality of appointment is rare in the annals of public institutions, it is not wholly without precedent. For one hundred years during the Middle Ages, Christendom beheld the edifying spectacle of rival Popes, one in Rome and the other in Avignon, each periodically addressing the whole body of the faithful as if he alone were the true viceregent of heaven upon earth. Yet so far as I can read, the cause of religion does not appear to have suffered from this division of authority, which assuredly added considerably to the stock of gaiety among the contemporary communities of unbelievers outside."

A letter to be " preserved" !

I remember well Sir Thomas's first Hallé Concert in Manchester in March 1912. At least I remember his walk to the conductor's desk, the immaculate " tails " and high starched collar, his leisurely progress and his side glance of tolerant recognition that an audience was present—(" and what an audience! "). A score had been placed on the music stand. He picked it up with his fingertips, as though it were unclean, and sent it sliding over the top of the concert " grand " piano, whence it proceeded by ricochet into the midst of the 'cellos. And twenty-seven years after this event of his baptism at a Hallé Concert, I was a witness of almost his last appearance for the society, at a concert in aid of the Hallé Orchestra Pension Fund. He, as president, was awarding medals commemorating long service to two retiring Hallé players. He addressed the audience in these words—" Ladies and Gentlemen, as I present these medals to two worthy members of an orchestra of great renown, and which you don't really deserve to have in Manchester, I am reminded of the occasion when the honour and privilege were mine to present the Gold Medal of the Royal Philharmonic Society to M. Pachmann . . . At this concert we were performing one of the Chopin piano concertos—I forget which—and Pachmann was playing with that felicity of touch now legendary; and I was conducting as well as it is humanly possible to conduct a Chopin Piano Concerto . . . In the middle of the slow movement, Pachmann stopped dead, stopped playing, and, leaning over the keyboard towards me, said 'Isn't it lofely?' And I replied, 'Indeed it is lovely, M. Pachmann—but would you mind going on?' " A star danced, surely, when Sir Thomas was born—and went out of the musical sky at his death.

During the 1914-1918 war, Sir Thomas guided the Hallé

Concerts safely through troublesome times, taking no fee for his services. Moreover, he produced opera in Manchester as it had never before, and has never since, been produced in this country in point of style. He also undertook to build an opera house in Manchester if the city would provide him with a site. A huge vacant space in Manchester's Piccadilly, where the Royal Infirmary had stood, an eye-sore and reproach, seemed to be the very spot. Of course, nothing came of Sir Thomas's flight of fancy. To-day the site in Manchester's Piccadilly is a bus station; and to-day Manchester hears about as much opera in a decade as Sir Thomas lavished on us, even though he didn't get his new opera house, in a few unforgettable weeks, year by year.

It was in Australia that I first got to know Sir Thomas as a friend should know a friend, by daily communion. He voyaged there in 1940, and I had been invited by Sir Keith Murdoch to join the staff of the "Herald" in Melbourne, mainly to write for his paper on Sir Thomas's concerts. One late autumn afternoon, I waited at the quay in Pyrmont in Sydney for Sir Thomas to emerge from the ship. As it was wartime, we were not allowed to go anywhere near the landing-stage. With me, as I waited, was William James, director of music of the Australian Broadcasting Corporation. The high buildings deprived us of the last warming rays of the setting sun. We grew cold; we shivered and wondered—what had happened to Sir

Thomas? A hundred and more passengers from the ship had gone by. We peered into every passing car. In vain. "We've missed him somehow," said James. At last Sir Thomas strolled into view, thickly overcoated. "Where have you been?" we naturally asked. "I have been retrieving a box of my cigars from my luggage in the hold." This was his first and only visit to Australia, and he took possession at once. In the Australia Hotel he had waiters, page-boys, and the manager himself, running around like lackeys. James then invited him to give an interview that night over the radio, myself the interviewer. I asked Sir Thomas to rehearse with me. He had not talked on the air before; nevertheless he declined to rehearse. "I prefer in these matters to improvise. Just you say a word or two, put any question you like to me, to start me off. After all, my dear fellow, listeners will want to hear me, not you . . ." So we went on the air without script, without preparation at all.

I began by asking: "Now, Sir Thomas, you are about to conduct orchestras entirely strange to you. Tell me, do you agree with the old saying that there are no good or bad professional orchestras, only good and bad conductors?" I breathed with relief; I could, I imagined, now sit back and be entertained, in common with all listening Australia, by half an hour of Sir Thomas . . . The fact is that for once in a lifetime he dried up. After a half a minute's silence—an eternity in time measured by radio—he snapped back at me. "What precisely do you mean?" Completely stunned, I repeated the question, adding by way of variation . . . " only good and bad conductors—I believe it was von Bülow who said it." " Did he really ? " responded Sir Thomas, sceptically, relapsing once more into sterile silence. Sweating heavily, I heaved the creaking wheel round again. " Do you intend to conduct much Mozart ? " " Whether I shall conduct, to use your phrase, much Mozart, depends on the condition of the orchestras here—about which you have given me no information whatsoever."

Somehow we temporised through half an hour of disconnected dialogue. I remember that he told me—and at the same time told countless invisible listeners—that I was talking too much. " Listeners want to hear me—not you. Please don't interrupt." At the end of the broadcast, as we were leaving the studio, he took me by the arm in his most friendly benevolent way and said, " There now—what did I tell you ? All talks over the air should be impromptu—unrehearsed." Next day I was asked by not a few friends. " Were you and Sir Thomas a little ' tight ' last night ? You certainly both sounded like it."

At Brisbane Sir Thomas rehearsed in a schoolroom. One of the pieces was the prelude to " Tristan und Isolde." Many of Australia's best instrumentalists were away at the war. A greying lady led the 'cellos, a music teacher. She drew her bow passionately, but her tone was quite excruciating. Her vibrato was the measure of the pressure she was applying to her phrasing. Sir Thomas stopped the orchestra suddenly, turned benignly to the greying schoolmistress 'cellist and said, " My dear, please don't take it so very much to heart."

The rehearsal was unmusical and empirical. I feared that at its outset, Sir Thomas's tour of Australia would abruptly end. To-morrow the balloon would go up, surely, with Sir Thomas cancelling all dates, and leaving Australia for good and all. But next morning when I saw him in his room at the hotel, he was as genial as ever in his dressing-gown, saying nothing of last night's frustrations. Then as we talked, the Brisbane manager of the Australian Broadcasting Corporation—and all the orchestras in Australia are controlled and directed by this body—entered the suite. " Ah, Sir Thomas," he said, " I'm sorry about last night's rehearsal. But don't worry. I have been speaking to headquarters in Sydney over the phone. And I'm pleased to say that they have instructed me to let you have two extra rehearsals." " That's very kind of you," beamed Sir Thomas, " very kind indeed. But, my dear fellow, I don't think I'll accept your generous offer of extra rehearsals—they'll only get worse." Shrewd psychology. The concert was the best Brisbane had ever heard. Sir Thomas bewitched the orchestra into very musical playing.

The Australian orchestras took him to heart; not so everybody of the public. In England we have revelled in Sir Thomas's speeches at a concert's end, revelled in his flagellations by word of mouth of our musical and cultural shortcomings. He, of course, told Australian audiences that they were ignorant, that he had seen more intelligent faces in the remoter villages of Bulgaria. Students of the magnificent University of Perth, in Western Australia, reacted so touchily to Sir Thomas's diatribes that on the eve of his departure from Perth by sea, they boarded the ship, and entered his cabin with the intention of cutting off his beard. But they found Sir Thomas asleep face down on his pillow. Afraid to wake him, they stealthily glided away, scissors and all.

Every day for three or more months I talked and lunched and dined with him. By daily contact our relationship changed from that of conductor and critic to friendship. I had, in England, spent many hours with him, as will be gathered from my foregoing pages. This Australian journey threw us together constantly, and the fact that we were more or less strangers to a very large continent helped to consolidate an acquaintance already of some dozen years' duration. I had to swallow many a dish of his sarcasm, no doubt; but I had long since realised that mischief and impishness, never unkindness or malice, inspired his verbal assaults on me. I discovered in him a simplicity which he never showed to the world at large. Also a certain loneliness. Not that he was given to idle mooning about in his moments of solitude. Many times have I come upon him, almost unannounced, on trains and in hotels, and I can't recollect that ever I found him unoccupied. He was always reading a score, a book, a newspaper. It was, in fact, recurrent attacks of an innate feeling of personal loneliness, even of something in him unfulfilled, that drove him to ceaseless absorption in work or study. He escaped from himself this way.

In Sydney he asked me at very short notice to dine with him. He was, for a change, not now in a hotel; he had rented a handsome flat overlooking the incredibly beautiful harbour. As I entered the flat—he himself opened the door, for he was alone—I was assailed by a strong smell of something burning. I drew his attention to it. Yes, he had just noticed it himself, after leaving the inner room in order to open the door to let me in. "Come," he said, "let us investigate. The aroma issues from the pantry." And in the pantry a mess of milk covered stove and floor. "Ah," he remarked, as though some scientific revelation was being vouchsafed to him. "I was boiling some milk—a panful. I have all my life been under the impression that milk was a substance which took an hour at least to boil. Very strange, isn't it?" If I had been a woman I should have fallen in love with him on the spot, if only to "mother him."

He did not of course travel to and through Australia unaccompanied. With him was Miss Dora Labette, the soprano singer, whom Sir Thomas presented during the 1930s at Covent Garden as the "new Italian nightingale Lisa Perli." For many years she had appeared on the concert platform in every city in Great Britain. The metamorphosis of Miss Labette into Signorina Perli is another joyous episode I shall later discuss in its right context.

On this evening of the scalded milk Miss Dora had gone to Government House representing Sir Thomas at some social event there. Sir Thomas avoided such ordeals. So, for this particular evening a meal had been improvised by Dora—" a cold collation "—as Sir Thomas called it, with champagne. Outside the wide open window of the room the Australian twilight was falling, deep purple over the bay. The lights of distant Bondi Beach were bright and steady. Sydney's " Show Boat " went over the water. This scene is fixed in my memory. Sir Thomas in his dressing-gown, his cigar smoke going straight up. I don't know why we remember certain scenes and moments, some of them of everyday commonplace incidence, and forget others. Sir Thomas was in excellent form, having been tuned especially by the revelation to him of the incalculable behaviour of milk on an electric stove.

He spoke of the Restoration dramatists—" I am preparing an edition and editing a definitive edition," he said, " of all of them, the greatest in any literature in the world." He would say things like this, as the spirit moved him; then forget them. But during his Australian tour, he dictated for hours to Dora; there may be writings by him hidden somewhere. Unfortunately the nuance and accent which flavoured his dictations were seldom carried over by him to the printed page. Herein lies the danger of dictation; the speaker, if he is a good speaker, is deceived into thinking that the sound of his voice will be reproduced on paper. I am sure that Sir Thomas's seductive voice would bewitch a passage of printed prose as anonymous as the following quotation from his autobiography, " A Mingled Chime " . . . " In general company he (Delius) loved passionately to provoke highly controversial discussions on every subject imaginable; and in these matters he was seen at his social best; for his uncanny gift of penetrating the heart of the matter and hitting the nail on the very centre of its head often gained him the advantage over men who had the reputation of being experts in their particular calling." I can imagine that this stately procession of clichés would sound, with Sir Thomas's vocal diction, sonorous and Augustan as the prose of Edmund Burke. Anthologists, collecting the sayings of Sir Thomas, are prone to forget that to reproduce them verbatim on paper, some subtlety of written evocation is necessary. The saying must emerge from a living situation.

It was in this magical scene in Sydney that Sir Thomas sat down at the piano and challenged me to identify musical quotations as he played them. For a while I didn't fare too badly, until he gave me his naughtiest glance. "One hundred pounds to a Henry Clay cigar that I now stump you, run you out, and take your middle wicket in consecutive balls! In other and plainer words, what is this?" I was indeed stumped, etc. I could name the period. The turn of the 18th to the 19th century. "Is it by that very much neglected composer Anon?" I asked. The music he was playing was from E.T.A. Hoffman's opera "Undine." "Please go on," I asked. He played Hoffman for at least half an hour. At this time I didn't know Hoffman had composed anything. Was he making it all up? To this day I have been unable to procure a score of "Undine." Sir Thomas assured me that he also had never seen the score. "I heard the opera during one of my visits to Germany," he said, "Only once?" I asked. "No, twice," he said.

Next day he was invited by the mayor of Sydney to sail in a launch to view the inner harbour, a dream-scape of colour. He dressed himself to suit the occasion, a nautical peaked cap and brass buttons on a bluish coat. Where had he got these garments from? Only a telescope was missing. The mayor especially wished to show him the Sydney bridge. Now the Sydney bridge is a fine sight seen from a distance, but the mayor had the launch directed exactly under it. "Now, Sir Thomas," asked the mayor triumphantly, "what do you think of our bridge?" Sir Thomas looked straight upward, risking a crick in the neck. The launch tossed a little; and Sir Thomas replied, "I don't think I like it at all. Why don't you have it removed?" "Removed," bear in mind, not "destroyed" or "dismantled." And he wondered why he was not exactly popular in Australia.

He did not go out of his way to adapt himself to a strange setting. "Brash," he called it. He wouldn't accept the rather fulsome hospitality offered to him. The Australians, in the mass, are friendly and hearty; Sir Thomas didn't enjoy heartiness that slapped him on the shoulder. Still, in his tolerant moments, he saw the fun which the Australian want of inhibitions generated day by day. "When I called one morning at the headquarters of the Australian Broadcasting Corporation," he reported, "a pretty girl in the outer office received me. She was heavily 'made-up,' in Technicolor, so to say. To be approachable I said to her, 'You are looking very handsome this morning, my dear.' And she replied, 'Ow, Sir Thomas, be your ha-ige.'" On the whole, the orchestras, in spite of the wartime demands on many good players, pleasantly surprised him. Curiously enough, though I can recall in detail countless performances in England conducted by Sir Thomas, only one or two of his concerts in Australia remain clearly in my mind. In Sydney he achieved a truly brilliant interpretation of the "Symphonie Fantastique" of Berlioz, and a very musical G minor symphony of Mozart in Melbourne. At Melbourne he began a rehearsal by asking the first violin the name of the main item in the programme. "The 'Pathétique' symphony." "'The Pathétique?'—ah, well, gentlemen, let us see what we can do to cheer it up."

The day before he departed from Australia, he called me to his room and flabbergasted me by saying that he had arranged for a cabin to be reserved for me on the ship which was taking him to America. "But," I gasped, "I have no intention of leaving Sydney just now and going to America." "Do you propose," he said, "do you propose to stay in this barbarous country all your life?" He was truly hurt at my refusal to submit to his whim. It was natural for him to think that he could take command of other people's inclinations and destinies.

We did not meet again for five or six years; then on the

last morning of the year, a telephone message to my club invited me to lunch. I didn't wish to lunch that day because I preferred to keep myself fresh for a New Year's Eve party. But an invitation from Sir Thomas was always a royal command, brooking no denial. So I went to the Aperitif Grill in Jermyn Street at one o'clock; and at once announced that as my "tummy" was rather out of order (it wasn't, of course) I would not eat much, or take wine at all. Whereat Lady Betty, his recently new wife, asked me, "Is it very painful?—perhaps it's appendicitis." "Good lord, no, Lady Betty," I said, "just a touch of indigestion, so I'll take only a bit of fish and some Perrier water." "But," persisted Lady Betty, "I wouldn't neglect it if I were you. You should have an X-ray examination." "But really," I repeated, "it's nothing at all, nothing serious, just a touch of 'wind.'" "All the same," Lady Betty implored, "you should see a specialist at once. Only the other week a very dear friend of mine——" And now Sir Thomas spoke, in a voice a little tired, "This conversation," he said, "doesn't seem to be developing."

He could not bear to be bored. All conversation in his presence simply had to develop. Sometimes, with his relish of a monologue, he might bore his listeners. He could not, apparently, bore himself. Not once in my experience of him did he engage in small talk. As soon as he met anybody he would go to the heart of some matter, usually to the heart of controversy. I never heard him discuss religion or politics. In hours and hours of talk with him

I cannot recall that he once mentioned chamber music. Opera, symphony, all sorts of instrumental and vocal music but not chamber music. His reading was considerable in classical and English and French literature. He knew Dickens by heart, but ranked "Vanity Fair" of Thackeray the greatest English novel of his period. He was as sceptical of contemporary writing as he was of the latest composition. I guessed that in politics he was a conservative—with freedom to be against the Government whatever its colour or party. He loved good food and good wine, and his cigars, but not to excess. No alcohol had power over his quick balanced mind. I was taken aback when he reflected one day on his career: "Do you know, I sometimes wonder if I haven't wasted myself to some degree by giving myself almost wholly to music. For music does not ever encourage abstract thinking or pungency of comment or dialectical agility. Perhaps I was really born for the legal profession."

I pointed out that in music he was an absolutist, that he had no patience with music which carried extra-musical significances, and that also he had no patience with conductors, or any other performer, who found an argument, a dialectic or the faintest hint of a metaphysic in music. He didn't seek beyond the notes and the forms of music for some inner meaning. Often he gave me the impression that he was not so much the "possessed" artist in music as the connoisseur, collecting composers as he collected his furniture and plate. He fondled music, handled it carefully and dotingly—unless it was of the sort that protested too much, assaulted fastidiousness of taste and sensitivity. "Mahler? Wagner? Bruckner?" he would say, cross-examining me. "They are not civilised. Mahler exposes his self-pity; Wagner, though a tremendous genius, gorged music, like a German who overeats. And Bruckner was a hobbledehoy who had no style at all. All three of them knew nothing about poise or modesty. Even Beethoven thumped the tub; the Ninth symphony was composed by a kind of Mr. Gladstone of music."

All that doesn't imply that he was at all short of masculinity, red corpuscles. He could ride roughshod over his dislikes, people or compositions. Given the impulse from the right source, his musical energy—(his physical energy too!)—concentrated into artistic and proportionate shapes. His interpretation of the "Requiem Mass" of Berlioz has seldom been equalled for emotional intensity and sure-minded control of the outlines. His temperament and intelligence responded more readily to Latin than to German stimulations, æsthetic or other. Sometimes he gave his conscience a holiday. At Liverpool an inordinately heavy programme was goading the orchestra to open rebellion, especially as Sir Thomas prolonged the interval. The concert was taking place on the eve of the world's greatest steeplechase. When Sir Thomas returned to the platform he immediately sensed the temper of his players—and the next work to tackle was the "great C major" symphony of Schubert. Sir Thomas extended his arms, the baton militant. "Now, gentlemen," he said, "now for the Grand National." The performance was magnificent. One gust of his humour dispersed all animosities.

He was not, as I say, liked or admired by everybody while he was the spruce disdainful Mr. Thomas Beecham. He was suspected of Dandyism and, in fact, he was the last of the Dandies. He kept audiences waiting at his concerts. In Manchester, during one of his opera seasons there, he kept the audience waiting half an hour for a performance of Isidore de Lara's "Naïl." In those years his manners at a symphony concert did not appeal to the taste of the Establishment of British music. The music critic of the "Manchester Guardian"—Samuel Langford—took him to task on account of his acrobatic gestures as he conducted. At one concert his baton flew from his hand and nearly impaled the first trombone. Moreover, he was suspected of "amateurism"—long before Toscanini actually called him an "amateur." A complex character!—Falstaff, Puck and Malvolio all mixed up, each likely to overwhelm the others. Witty, then waggish; supercilious, then genial, kindly, and sometimes cruel; an artist in affectation yet somehow always himself. Lancashire in his bones, yet a man of the world. Rachmaninoff told a friend that he was unhappy about a forthcoming concert. "The conductor—so-and-so—he has no temperament. It is always so in England. Too many the English gentlemens." "But," his friend pointed out "last year you said your concert with Sir Thomas Beecham was one of the best and happiest of your life." "Ah," rejoined Rachmaninoff, "but Sir Thomas is not one of your English gentlemens."

In the prime of his life and career, Sir Thomas was as closely associated with Manchester as with London or anywhere else. During the 1914-1918 war he kept the city's music alive by the sparkle, vivacity, and sway of his personality. His concerts with the Hallé Orchestra and his opera productions in Quay Street elevated the city far above provincial levels. Until he dominated the scene Manchester's music was mainly of German extraction, as we have noted already and will probably note again. Richter had not served Manchester in a backward-looking way. He conducted all the symphonic poems of Richard Strauss in one season at a time when—*mirabile dictu!*—Strauss was considered as "modern," iconoclast and unmusical as any later Schönberg, Webern, or Boulez. Stanford went so far as to compose a musical satire of Strauss—"An Ode to Discord." Ernest Newman abjured us to listen to Strauss "horizontally" while the battle-section of "Ein Heldenleben" was played. It is nowadays generally forgotten that Strauss came to renown or notoriety in this country exclusively on the strength of his symphonic poems. Outside London "Der Rosenkavalier," "Salome" and "Elektra" were little known here.

But Richter's enterprise ended with the "progressive German composers." It is true that he was the first conductor to put Elgar on the musical map, the reason being, I fancy, that in Elgar he heard here and there the echo of his own native musical language. To a deputation of

Manchester's youthful *avant garde*, demanding some representation at the Hallé Concerts of modern French music, Richter replied, "Zthere iss no mod'n F-french Musik."

Beecham brought pagan allurements to the Hallé, non-"classical"—Scene IV of Act II of Delius's "A Village Romeo and Juliet," Stravinsky's "Firebird" suite, Borodin's "Polovtsian Dances," all in the same programme. Between the two wars he naturally modulated to a conversation indicative of the fact that he was now old enough to put behind him childish things. But never would he desert Delius. On the "classical" side he discovered Haydn for English ears. He even proposed introducing to Manchester Stravinsky's "Le Sacre du Printemps"; but the orchestral parts went astray. The Hallé Concerts Committee asked for a substitute piece at short notice. Beecham suggested a Beethoven symphony. No; already the season's programme had included enough Beethoven. They asked Sir Thomas to conduct Mendelssohn's "Italian" symphony. "Impossible," replied Sir Thomas, "quite impossible, with only two rehearsals." "But," argued the committee, "you were content with two rehearsals for 'Le Sacre.'" "Quite so," said Sir Thomas blandly, "I could play 'Le Sacre' well enough after two rehearsals. For the 'Italian' symphony five at least is absolutely necessary."

His creation of the London Philharmonic Orchestra absorbed him and his time in the 1930s; consequently his appearances in Manchester became intermittent. After the resignation of Sir Hamilton Harty in 1933 as the permanent conductor of the Hallé Concerts, the orchestra declined in its ensemble. Another permanent conductor was needed, but the Hallé Society were reluctant to appoint one for fear of losing Sir Thomas's presence altogether. And Sir Thomas scared the society by attacking the B.B.C., forecasting that broadcasting would keep people away from concerts. As critic of the "Manchester Guardian," in Manchester in the 1930s, I pointed out week by week the falling away of the orchestra in unity of style. But my friendship with Sir Thomas, resumed soon after our argument about his "cuts" in "Der Rosenkavalier," was now apparently unclouded. I was vastly surprised and amused to learn from Michael Kennedy's history of the Hallé Concerts that in 1937 Sir Thomas wrote to the society stating "that he refused to conduct any concert to which Mr. Neville Cardus was invited." *Et tu*, Sir Thomas! And all the time I imagined my notices were generously kind about him. Never did he refer to this letter to the Hallé Society, demanding my excommunication, at any of my subsequent meetings with him, not even during our day by day, night by night expressions of brotherly love in Australia.

It was round about 1931 that he told me he was about to form a new orchestra in London. "But where," I asked, "where do you hope to find the players?—the B.B.C. Orchestra has taken the best." "Maybe," he admitted "the B.B.C. has indeed attracted the best known instrumentalists of Great Britain. But you'll see!" In 1932 the Royal Philharmonic Orchestra played for the first time at the Queen's Hall. The performance of the "Carnaval Romain" overture of Berlioz was staggeringly brilliant. A highly finished performance of Mozart's "Prague" symphony almost jerked me from my seat when Sir Thomas brought in the D major principal theme, after the introduction, at the same adagio tempo, instead of allegro. My notice next day called for some explanation of this curious treatment or maladjustment. In his flat in Hallam Street, and while he was still in bed, working on a score, he took away my breath (not for the first or the last time) by assuring me that his tempo for the main theme after the introduction was authentic. "You are probably acquainted only with the published score . . . but I have seen the original manuscript written by Mozart's own hand . . ." All the same, the next time he conducted the "Prague" symphony the theme in question was allegro all right and unmistakably. He was in a word, *capable de tout!*

Apart from some piano lessons in boyhood he was self-taught. He states the contrary in his biography, "A Mingled Chime," where he writes, "In public accounts of my career has frequently appeared the assertion that I am almost entirely self-taught and, beginning as a rank amateur, have attained a professional status with some difficulty after a long and painful novitiate. Nothing could be more remote from the truth. It is possible that at the age of twenty I might have failed to answer some of the questions in an examination paper set for boys of sixteen in a musical academy; but probably I should fail with equal success to-day; and I venture to say that a tolerable number of my most gifted colleagues would do no better. On the other hand, owing to my travels abroad and wider associations with musicians here and there, my miscellaneous fund of information was much more extensive than that of others of my age." For Sir Thomas, this is positively naïve. There was music of sorts in his St. Helens home; his father practised music "as a hobby." Sir Thomas substantially educated himself, as Elgar did, and Ernest Newman and Delius, perhaps the most cultured and influential figures in our music's history since Purcell.

He came down from Oxford after only a year or so there because, as he explained to me, "there was no musical life broad and humane enough. As for the rest of my studies at Oxford, they were not attractively conducted. And I could discover no mind or intelligence among my fellow undergraduates which didn't indicate permanent adolescence. In those days, even to-day in fact, the average University-educated Englishman is a case of arrested development, emotionally, æsthetically and sexually."

His own capacity for deep feeling was not often or obviously hinted at in his studied deportment away from the concert platform or desk at the opera. He gave unmistakable proof of it in my company only once, during one of the last evenings I spent with him alone, a few months after Lady Betty's sudden death. Speaking of her, he was obviously moved. "She was a wonderful comrade," he said.

" Comrade "—again the unexpected word. Is it to be wondered at that for all his usually detached and " superior " manner, his vanities, and the impression he gave that even his closest friend was not essential to his way of life—is it a wonder that he was, especially in his old age, very much liked, in fact very much loved? The orchestras didn't call him " Tommy " for nothing. When he was conducting in an American city where the " colour bar " held sway, he one day went into the segregated Negro community and was seen walking the streets in company with a little black girl, with her hand tightly clasped in his. He did nothing by halves, whether in a good or bad, kindly or waspish mood. On his eightieth birthday, at a lunch given in his honour in a London hotel, this is the way he finished his speech of thanks:

" Years are nothing. Thought and feeling—notably feeling—are all that matter. Say what you want to say, with firmness and conviction. The one thing that is really important, in playing, in conducting—yes, and even in misconducting—is this: whatever you do, do it with conviction."

A Conversation Piece

❧

N.C. THERE IS A GENERAL IDEA CIRCULATING TO the effect that you are not interested in contemporary music, and seldom go out of your way to study it.

Sir T. As a fact I have studied this kind of music—atonal, serial or what have you . . . It is true that so far I have been unable to interest myself in it. The fault, I assure you, is not mine. But I repeat, I have certainly tried. And I have all my life examined the newest scores. Once on a time my programmes were looked at askance by the conservative-minded. I was the first conductor in this country to present Stravinsky with some understanding and sympathy. I was attracted to his music because it corrected Teutonic tendencies towards adiposity and flatulence. Stravinsky's music, after we had been overdosed by Wagner and Brahms and the rest of the Germans, was a sedative for the "hangover."

N.C. And to-day?

Sir T. To-day Stravinsky seems to me an extraordinary case of self-metamorphosis, if you follow me. His style, his way of composing is unmistakable. But there is behind his façade of ingenious notes and patterns no continuous personality. The young scribes in the capital cities of Europe and America are impressed because Stravinsky is versatile. No great composer, no artist working in any medium, can even over a long stretch of years, change his style as easily as all that. Yes—I know what you are about to say. You are about to tell me—please don't interrupt—that Stravinsky's most recent productions are as unmistakably by Stravinsky as " Petrouchka " and " Le Sacre." You are—or were—about to tell me that his ' Symphony in Three Movements," and his " Canticum Sacrum " are signed Stravinsky beyond all manner of doubt whatsoever. It is a trick of technical legerdemain. Stravinsky, a superb professional, knows all the tricks of the trade. No composer has had a finer musical intelligence and taste than Stravinsky's. Unfortunately, intelligence and taste are not enough in themselves for the creation of enduring art, especially if intelligence and taste don't grow up. I do not find in Stravinsky's newest productions convincing signs that he has arrived at wisdom, even yet. He is still a remarkable and refreshing innovator or, rather, a ringer of fresh changes. As a creative force he has, I fear, been a spent force for years. Naturally he appeals—he always has appealed—to the young and emotionally inexperienced. He betrayed his Russian origins. Now he is a composer for the fashionable coteries—entertaining, clever as a hundred musical monkeys. But I, once an ardent admirer of Stravinsky, find him now sometimes boring. I am not sure that Cecil Gray wasn't right when he described Stravinsky as Diaghilev's greatest creation.

N.C. And Schönberg?

Sir T. A very remarkable musical explorer. But artists who are possessed by genius are not free to concentrate on research and experiments. The possessed genius needs at hand an already organised basic language. He may add to it here and there, give it a new direction; but his vocabulary must be a standard vocabulary . . . For me, much of Schönberg is unintelligible, and remains unintelligible, much as I study his scores . . . Yet all, or nearly all, your youngish colleagues profess to understand Schönberg as though they had assimilated him with their mothers' milk. A year or two ago when " Moses and Aaron " was about to be produced, two eminent musicians attended the rehearsal, a famous composer and a famous conductor. At the end of the final rehearsal, one of these eminent musicians said to the other, " do you understand it? " And the other replied " No—not all of it." But your young colleagues have written about " Moses and Aaron " as though the music were as intelligible to them as the next Brahms symphony.

N.C. Perhaps you have heard the story of Schönberg at a rehearsal of one of his late-period works. One of the instrumentalists lost his way for several bars. But Schönberg offered no correction—so the conductor asked Schönberg, " Meister, do you mean to say that you can't follow your own music? " And Schönberg answered, " Not always—but my grandchildren will."

Sir T. Very good, but I fancy you have made it up yourself. Schönberg of course was a sincere musician. It is his young critics who are insincere, or at any rate, who " *pretend*," for fear of appearing not up-to-date. There's another point—it is easier to describe the technical apparatus of a new composition than it is to write about its æsthetic significance.

Not that I admit for a moment that music is a language translatable into words. But a critic, in order to be readable, must seem always to be referring a great work to some imaginative or emotional experience. If he writes in the jargon of technique, the majority even of his most educated readers won't understand—while the musical specialist is able to find out these esoteric matters for himself.

N.C. But more and more young people are giving ear to Schönberg and the others known as " modern."

Sir T. It is natural for young people to run after the latest thing. We live in an age of science and mechanics. There has never been an age, since the period of Attila, as unæsthetic as this we now live in. The young people being, as I say, æsthetically and emotionally inexperienced, respond to the " new " music much as they respond to a " new " machine. There is also another reason to account for the current neglect of a " romantic " composer, unless he happens to have been established for centuries; but I will refrain from dwelling upon this reason, except to say that if the tendency I have in mind is not soon checked a man will not know which way to turn. Reverting to the present fashionable composers, I have recently made an experiment—I have carefully noted, over a period of nearly a year, the London critics' printed opinions of Schönberg, Berg, Webern and Stravinsky, and not once have I read a word of really adverse judgment of any of them, not one word. Apparently these composers cannot go wrong; every bar they have written is, according to the published verdicts of London's young critical lions, faultless.

These critics are like party politicians. They do not seem to know that a sure sign of genius is an ebb and flow of his creative energy.

N.C. Do you hope for a future for your favourite Delius?

Sir T. Not until there is an end to the reaction against romanticism—to use the present-day stupid label fixed by these critics on all works of art which aim at a personal expression of feeling and sensibility in terms of melody, harmony and musical diction which can be understood by the average educated listener . . . Perhaps a universal disaster—another war—might bring back a condition of affairs in which a man, even a young man, would really have to behave like a *man.* In some such holocaust, no coterie in the arts could survive. Vents would be needed for the expression of all sorts of emotion. As to Delius . . . the best of his music might, during or after such a world-shaking-up, command attention. But I am doubtful. Frankly, I don't think our Western civilisation will ever again—at least, not for a century of time—be refined and civilised in Delius's way.

N.C. By that argument, Sir Thomas, artists to-day are wise then to explore a new language, new symbols, in which to crystallise a new æsthetic, a new means of giving artistic shape to their reactions to life.

Sir T. I have no objection to industrious pioneers who strive to reshape art-forms and extend the language of the arts. Rameau was doing that sort of thing nearly two hundred years ago. Who except a musicologist ever listens to Rameau to-day? A musicologist, by the way, is a man who can read music but can't hear it . . . Talking of Delius—whose musical brain, *his musical brain*, my dear fellow—was keen and strong, so much so that compared with it nearly all his critics are musical morons . . . talking of Delius, the other day, I read an account of " A Mass of Life " by one of your junior colleagues. From his point of view it was intelligent enough, though his prose style left a taste of sawdust in my mouth. He wrote to the effect that Delius's " disciples " don't regard " A Mass of Life " as one of Delius's best works. I myself certainly regard it as his best, so do countless other musicians. Mahler, you may be interested to learn, was very much attracted to the " Mass " in his later years; and after Richard Strauss had heard a performance of the work, he told me that he hadn't suspected that anybody was composing anything so good at the time—except himself. Your immature scribe also stated that " the solemn naïve philosophy selected from Nietzsche's ' Also sprach Zarathustra ' is even more distant from our present mentality and more irrelevant to the spiritual problems of our age than that of the composer's other poet, Walt Whitman." Is the test of a composition written more than half a century ago that it should have relevance to the spiritual problems of our present age? It is strange—is it not?—that in our present-day civilisation, which is more brutal and insensitive than any since the darkest of the Dark Ages—strange that the critics should so frequently be demanding that writers, poets, composers and painters should keep themselves up-to-date in their ideas and feelings. Whenever I listen on Sundays to those curious wild-fowl " The Critics," over the radio, I am constantly hearing some voice dismissing a famous nineteenth-century genius because, in the speaker's opinion, his works are "dated." For example, Ibsen, the other Sabbath morning, had the term applied to him. Such nonsense I never hear on the Continent. Only in London, which is now a centre of pretentiousness in affairs of the arts and of the mind, is this kind of uncritical belittlement allowed a public utterance. Criticism of the arts in London, taken by and large, ends in a display of suburban omniscience which sees no farther than into the next-door garden.

N.C. But haven't most of the geniuses been ahead of their time?

Sir T. As far as I have been able to study the doings of the most far-seeing of geniuses, I am led to believe that they have invariably expressed themselves in terms more or less understood by average educated listeners of their own period. Many of them would speedily have been disposed of by their patrons, had they got out of a patron's power of comprehension.

N.C. Beethoven was at one time considered fit for the madhouse.

Sir T. Perhaps at one time, perhaps at many times, Beethoven *was* fit for the madhouse. We must remember, too, that performances in those distant years, were often incapable of doing justice to a new work. And few means existed then whereby a new work could become familiar to the public. Scores were not easily acquired. And there was no radio, no gramophone. "Tristan und Isolde," for instance, was immediately revealed as a masterpiece to those musicians who were able to study the score. I fancy that I myself can read a score with some facility. And I am capable of flexible reactions of my musical intelligence. As I have said, I have for years studied the scores of composers who, it appears, are entirely intelligible to many of your young colleagues. These scores continue to baffle me . . . What, in the way of musical antennæ, do these young men possess that I don't . . .? To refer again to the gentlemen —and ladies—who perform each Sabbath morning. They are familiar with all sorts of schools of art, with every period of literature. They have seen every film, every play. And they lay down the law on every known technique. Each of these critics pontificates on how to write a play, how he (or she) could have improved on the structure of the third act of the production which he happens this week to be reviewing. Each advises playwrights, poets, cinema and film producers, painters and actors—advises them on points of craftsmanship, which really is a specialist's concern.

I move about pretty freely in London circles, but never have I met intellectual paragons of this kind anywhere. Where do they live or hang out? Where did they acquire their encyclopædic knowledge? I am not uninstructed myself in painting, for instance, yet I would not in the course of a national broadcast, put my opinion of an artist against that of, say, Mr. Eric Newton.

N.C. Of course you would. . . .

(*Quick curtain*)

Musician and Conductor

❦

THE MUSICAL SCENE IN THESE ISLES AT THE TIME of Beecham's coming of age was not populous or eventful. Elgar was struggling for recognition by an Establishment governed by the academics. Wagner could be heard annually at Covent Garden in an expensive highly social season. In the provinces, even in Manchester, hailed by Elgar as the nation's musical centre, the " Ring " was not produced until round about 1911. Stanford's " Sea Songs " were considered worthy to be performed at an important annual " Festival " of music. (" O Westward ho! for Trinidad! "). William Wallace (not the composer of " Maritana ") had written the first British symphonic poem in 1892, called " The Passage of Beatrice." Wallace was a Scot, an ophthalmic surgeon and as accomplished a painter as composer. A musical criticism of the period was dubious about certain " chromatic " passages in Leoncavallo's " Pagliacci." Frederic Hymen Cowen's " Fantasy of Life and Love " was actually played at a Hallé Concert in Manchester. Granville Bantock, shrewd and cosmopolitan enough to put his ear to the ground and catch strains of Rimsky-Korsakov and Strauss, divided his violins and caused his wind parts to make noises like " Scheherazade." As a consequence he was regarded by many British musicians as a more " progressive " composer than Elgar. " Das Land ohne Musik."

In Lancashire, Beecham's home-ground, there were many "Glee" Societies fal-lal-ling on winter nights. But I, nearing twenty years of age and a denizen of Manchester, considered myself lucky if I could hear, at a Hallé Concert, the prelude to "Tristan und Isolde" twice played by an orchestra in the course of two or three years. Curiously enough, in this time of musical desert, Manchester and Lancashire might well be treated to several weeks of opera within a twelve-month, presented by travelling companies, the Carl Rosa, the Moody Manners and Joseph O'Mara, peripatetic and sometimes lost tribes. The singing in these companies was excellent; E. C. Hedmont ("Tannhäuser") Arthur Winkworth ("Wolfram") Doris Woodall ("Carmen"). To-day, for all the efforts of Arts Councils, the provincial cities of England are not as well-off for chances to hear opera as I was in Manchester half a century ago. These opera companies, kept solvent by performances of "The Bohemian Girl" and "Faust" on Saturday nights, tilled a soil from which Sir Thomas garnered rich produce later on—and only—a decade later on.

Sir Thomas astonished London when he chose "The Bohemian Girl" as the opera he wished to conduct at one of his last (if it was not the last) appearances at Covent Garden. "We owe much to Balfe," he said, "and, anyhow, the 'Bo Girl,' a ballad opera, should be perpetuated in England, as 'Czar and Zimmerman' is perpetuated in Germany." But after one or two nights spent conducting "The Bo Girl," he handed over the baton, as he put it, "to one of my hirelings."

He prepared himself for the bounty shortly to come to him, and to the rest of us, by wandering over the Continent listening to opera everywhere. It was the heyday of Wagner, and he heard little else but Wagner. Hence, possibly, the subsequent reaction on his part against Wagner. Strangely and sadly, he didn't go to Vienna, where he could have seen and heard Mahler. When I once reproached him for missing this golden opportunity, he said that from all he had been told of Mahler he wouldn't have enjoyed his conducting very much—" Obviously Mahler conducted egoistically." Which, coming from Sir Thomas, was rich indeed.

At the turn of the present century lessons with Charles Wood encouraged him to try his hand at the composition of an opera. He wrote his own libretto. He then met Luigi Illica, part author of the libretti of " La Bohème " and " Tosca " of Puccini. With Illica he planned another opera based on the life of Christopher Marlowe. In his autobiography he tells us nothing of the fate of these two attempts at creation. The libretto of the first surely was worth " preserving." He never spoke to me of any ambition on his part to compose an opera, not even when I told him I had been present, as a critic, at a production of " The Merchant of Venice," an opera composed by his son Adrian, who set to music every word of Shakespeare's play. It absorbed as much time in performance as " Götterdämmerung." The opera was in the ballad style with spoken dialogue. Sir Thomas asked me to read to him my review of the performance and I can still see, with my mind's eye, his face, as I quoted from my article the following sentence: "Mr. Beecham's adventure with Shakespeare has already provoked the disapproval of elderly critics . . . but one cannot quite see how any harm is to come. Let the opera turn out tolerable and all of us will have been done some good. Let the opera turn out bad and the benefit will be the composer's—since operas of any sort are best out of the system of a growing youth."

In Manchester in 1912, I saw, heard and experienced, Beecham's conducting for the first time, from the gallery of the Theatre Royal. Spruce and debonair, stiff as the high starched collar round his neck, he conducted a concert —and why it had to be given in the Theatre Royal and not in the Hallé Orchestra's home, the Free Trade Hall, I am at a loss to explain. Of this auspicious concert I remember only the performance of Wagner's "Faust" overture, how the soaring "Gretchen" melody went up as though visibly into the air. During Sir Thomas's old age he cajoled or coaxed orchestras into fine playing. In the rising temperature of early manhood he frequently dragooned them, with a ferocity of physical jerks and of voice. "Louder! Louder!" he would shout to obtain the crescendo of his heart's desire. In his early thirties he somehow contrived to look quite tall on the concert platform; at any rate, he gave no impression of a man slight of inches. He was then slender; gossip whispered that he wore stays. Also gossip, in more than a whisper, said that if he had not been rich enough to buy his way into prominence in London's musical scene, he wouldn't have been able to get a start at all, not with our best professional orchestras. It is true that he did, to a most expensive extent, buy his way—and justified the confidence he placed in himself, from the first of his steps forward.

Between 1909 and 1914 his fame as a conductor increased by leaps—keeping pace, in fact, with his notoriety as a man. The Establishment distrusted his wit and his " West End " flavours. In 1909 he produced Ethel Smyth's " The Wreckers " at His Majesty's. Beerbohm Tree, akin in wit to Beecham, actually permitted performances of opera on his own stage, in his own theatre. Tree was so jealous of His Majesty's that once he hailed a taxi and, asked by the driver where he wanted to go, said, " I'll direct you. Do you imagine I am going to pronounce the name of my beautiful theatre in a hired cab? " In the summer of 1911, Beecham really got into his stride, renting Covent Garden and introducing to London Strauss's " Elektra," which he conducted from memory; Delius's " A Village Romeo and Juliet " and reviving, of all things, Sullivan's " Ivanhoe " with its " Ho! Jolly Jenkins " Wardour Street quaintness. A few months later, again at His Majesty's, he produced and conducted " Cosî fan tutte," " Seraglio," Strauss's " Feuersnot," Stanford's " Shamus O'Brien " and Massenet's " Werther." And in the autumn of the same year he produced " Fidelio," " Don Giovanni " and Strauss's " Salome." Little was known then of Mozart's operas in this country; certainly next to nothing was known of " Così fan tutte " in England, or even in Germany and Austria. In fact this was one of the first performances of " Così fan tutte " London had heard. As Sir Thomas has himself written in his Autobiography—and written beautifully, " ' Così fan tutte ' is a long summer day spent in a cloudless land by a Southern Sea . . ." During the first night of " Elektra," the actor playing the part of the Young Slave mistook his cue and came on the stage considerably in advance of his proper time. He more or less extricated himself from the embarrassing position, stealing into the wings and hoping he had not been observed. When, at the right moment, he appeared again, Sir Thomas, riding the whirlwind of a climax, whispered to his first violin, " Albert—have we not seen this gentleman before this evening or am I suffering a delusion ? " In saying this he didn't miss a demi-semi-quaver of his firm control. Beecham's conducting of " Elektra " has not yet been surpassed for intensity and drive and continuous mastery of control.

Beecham chose for his Salome a Finnish artist, Aino Akte, young, beautiful, slim and daringly seductive. She horrified the authorities and audiences attending a Festival of Music in Birmingham by singing the closing scene of " Salome " in her stage dress and vivid make-up. I shall die in the belief that Sir Thomas arranged this bare-faced (to say the least) assault on Birmingham moral susceptibilities—to get " something of his own back " after Birmingham's silent reception of him on the occasion when he said to the orchestra, "Let us pray." Why shouldn't the closing scene of "Salome" be sung and played at a Birmingham Musical Festival? "'Salome,'" Sir Thomas argued, with an appropriate grimace, "is a Scriptural work, isn't it?"

In 1911 and 1912 he brought to London the Russian ballet, which took the town by storm. He conducted Stravinsky's "Petrouchka." Hence, until the outbreak of war in 1914, London, thanks wholly to Sir Thomas, was the most exciting and multitudinous and most multi-coloured centre in the world for opera and ballet. In succession he enchanted London with fruits rare and voluptuous. Such temptations to feed on sensuous delights had never before watered the mouths of London audiences: "Der Rosenkavalier," "Boris Godounov" with Chaliapin, "Ariadne" (the earlier version) with Beerbohm Tree as Jourdain; Rimsky-Korsakov's "Coq d'Or," Borodin's "Prince Igor," Ravel's "Daphnis and Chloe," "Le Rossignol" of Stravinsky. London has not since known the like of these glamorous nights. On the stage, maybe, they have been equalled in style, but not in range or in truly magical sway of personality. Besides, the brilliance and opulence on the stage were reflected in the audiences and thrown back again to the stage in flashes of beauty, elegance and wealth.

The war of 1914-1918 did not daunt or curb Sir Thomas's activities or his idealism. It was now that I came really to experience his conjurations; for he made Manchester a centre. At the Opera House in Quay Street, he lavished unforgettable seasons on us. He gathered together a company of singers and artists which, I swear, has had few equals, even at Glyndebourne or Salzburg. He was scornful to me when I missed, in later years, a Beecham opera night so that I could attend the first of all performances at Glyndebourne. " So you preferred Christie's Minstrels? " he leered. I have written in another place—(" Second Innings ") how young Mancunians hung on to every note (remember, again, there was no radio for us then), hung on from congested places, jammed in the alcoves of the pit, bottoms sore on the hard uncushioned seats of the gallery, while Beecham, whom we likened to a wizard over a cauldron of orchestral charms in the darkened theatre, wafted into our senses the magic of his baton. And the orchestra was our own Hallé. Ah, bliss was it then to be alive, when we could feel night by night that "*Jugend ist Trunkenheit ohne Wein!* "—which in good English if poor Goethe, could read as " Youth is intoxication without the need of wine."

In Manchester I heard " Parsifal " for the first time; but Sir Thomas did not conduct. I cannot recall that he ever conducted this music-drama; indeed he was no more to be associated with " Parsifal " than Noël Coward with the Oberammergau Passion Play. He made records from " Parsifal," not lingering over the " Good Friday " scene in the manner of Weingartner, whose tempi at a Covent Garden performance of " Parsifal " in 1938 was so slow that Ernest Newman, sitting in front of me, whispered in my ear, " Before this ' Good Friday ' is over it'll be Easter Monday."

But if Sir Thomas was not the first conductor to waft the " Parsifal " spell over me, his was the informing spirit behind the superb production at Quay Street, Manchester, in 1919. In a country, not yet opera-minded, with all our opera schooling and production vagrant and miscellaneous outside London, he conjured from the sullen air and soot-stained soil of Manchester, Wolverhampton and adjacent barren places, a number of singers possessing instinct for the stage; and he trained them into opera artists in the top class—a wonderful achievement which we simply cannot call back to mind often enough.

Eugène Goossens was conductor of my first " Parsifal," a young man in the mid-twenties, son of a father who, working nobly and almost anonymously for the Carl Rosa travelling operatic soup kitchen, prepared the soil. Already young Goossens had a technical equipment of prodigious range and fluency; I doubt very much if any other conductor in his mid-twenties has conducted " Parsifal," at all, let alone as masterfully as Goossens did in those halcyon years.

I admit that most of us who listened spellbound to this performance of " Parsifal " knew scarcely a note of it, though we had heard excerpts at the Hallé Concerts, Richter conducting. Consequently we were in no position truly to estimate the quality of the performance; we lacked standards. But we put our trust in Sir Thomas who had for years traversed Europe taking heed and taking notes in opera houses. A Viennese friend, living in Manchester, assured me that for fascination of scene and rounded beauty of musical style, "Parsifal" in Quay Street equalled "Parsifal" on the Opernring.

Frank Mullings, a name not known to-day, was by far the most poignant "Parsifal" of my experience. Not a tenor of honeyed tones; sometimes he shouted and strangled his voice. As an actor in opera, none except Chaliapin has come within miles of Mullings. As Parsifal he would stand watching the ceremony of the unfolding of the Grail. With his back to the audience, with not a movement and half-concealed in the shadows, he did not allow us to forget his presence. By some histrionic power he caused us to see through the eyes of Parsifal as well as through our own. We suffered with Amfortas and we were touched by the innocence of Parsifal. Other Parsifals, other tenors, might as well leave the stage during the unfolding of the Grail; perhaps they do leave it and we don't notice their departure.

Mullings as "Othello," in Verdi's opera, ran a good second, for magnificence of presence and intense characterisation to Chaliapin's 'Boris.' He was less demonstrative than Chaliapin. Mullings, a tall man and a big man, could incarnate Shakespeare's as well as Verdi's "Othello," and also make us feel his softness of nature, caught in the snare of his own elemental passion. In the scene with Iago in Act II, his ferocity was terrible; his Othello would do such things, but what they would be he knew not—

they would be the terror of the earth. Mullings, for all his ravening lust for revenge, understood proportion, knew the force of silence. As he entered the bedchamber of Desdemona, his silence pervaded the theatre from stage to topmost gallery. Mignon Nevada, the Desdemona to Mullings's Othello, confessed that his quietness often chilled her with something of apprehension. He had pride of carriage, too. Doom followed every step of his Tristan; when he appeared before Isolde in Act I his "Demand, lady, what you will"—("*Begehrt Herrin, was ihr wünscht*")—his hints of tragic fore-knowledge were overwhelming. "The value of Mullings's interpretation of Tristan," said Sir Thomas, "was that while the music was sung with greater vitality and tenderness than by any other artist I have heard, the whole part was endowed with a high nobility, an almost priestly exaltation of mood, and a complete absence of any wallowing in the sty of merely fleshly obsession. The general effect was one of rapt absorption in an other-worldly fantasy, hopeless of realisation on this earth; and this I believe to have been Wagner's own conception." Finely and truly spoken!

Mullings's voice could go painfully "off the line" at times; but his soft singing was extremely beautiful. Nobody has pronounced the English language with more than Mullings's locution. After a performance of "Tristan und Isolde," a Manchester music critic reported that Mullings had sung out of tune in the love duet. Sir Thomas, in a letter to the music critic's paper, pointed out that it was not Mullings who had been out of tune—it was Wagner.

In comic parts Mullings, like Chaliapin, could take away the breath of laughter. As Midas, in Bach's "Phoebus and Pan," his fooling was at one and the same time uproarious and classical. Yet, Beecham included in his repertory an example of Bach, allergic as he was to Bach as a whole. This repertory in a single season of a month, given in Manchester in Quay Street, might easily contain "Die Meistersinger," "Tristan und Isolde," "Boris Godounov," "Le Coq d'Or," "Louise," "Prince Igor," "Otello," "Falstaff," "Phoebus and Pan" and, of course, the best of Mozart.

The Beecham production of "The Marriage of Figaro" remains in my memory to-day, nearly fifty years after my last blissful participation in it, unparalleled. The setting was brilliant and charming. We would escape from the fog and slime of a winter night in Manchester and, after waiting in a growing excitement, our eyes and ears would be enchanted when the curtain went up and we saw sunshine flooding the stage from the garden outside. And our ears would take in the flowing delight of the music. No conductor has shared Beecham's secret of liberating the opening phrases, as Figaro measured the room. No Susanna has prattled with Desirée Ellinger's exquisite vanity—since her passing only Audrey Mildmay has approached the infectious and youthful vivacity of Desirée Ellinger in this scene, which is the most endearing and happy opening scene in all opera. The Figaro of Frederick Ranalow was Mozart's—not, as with most exponents of the part, Rossini's. Frederic Austin's Count had merely to cross the stage to give us a classical education; and the Countess of Agnes Nichols was all the melody and tender pathos of Mozart graciously mingled. No achievement in Sir Thomas's long life excelled this production, his evocation out of England's vacant operatic air, the assemblage of singers which, night after night, transformed a large ugly Manchester theatre into a cloudless heaven of felicity—Nevada, Nichols, Ranalow, Mullings, Percy Heming (a shattering Amfortas), Robert Radford (incomparable as the Father in "Louise"), Walter Hyde, Maurice D'Oisley, Miriam Licette (adorable as Louise), Norman Allin (one of the three best Amfortases of our time), Gladys Ancrum (I can hear her scream as Kundry as I write these lines), and Rosina Buckman, whose Cho-Cho San in "Madame Butterfly" nearly broke my heart. Her evocation of this part was quite marvellous, for she was an enormous woman physically. When asked by Sharpless to tell her age, her answer could easily have referred to her weight of flesh. Yet she was the only "Butterfly" in my experience who acted and played on the plane of the miniature according to the prompting of Puccini's music. Her tremulous, sadly hopeful tones, as in Act II she made herself look pretty—or prettier—to please Pinkerton on his return, the way she said she needed a little more carmine to hide the traces of tears—her art elevated and purified Puccini's score of all sentimentality. Samuel Langford, music critic of the "Manchester Guardian," protested against Buckman's fine arts in "Madame Butterfly"—"If I hear and see her again in the part I'll end up liking the opera."

Hyperbole? Was there no fault, no imperfection in these Manchester productions? They were scarcely noticed, because of the general tension, the tiptoe expectation of the packed audiences. We were present not at performances, not at reproductions of familiar things; we were receiving revelations. The radio-and-gramophone-fed musical public of to-day is not able to understand how these performances miraculously affected us in an age in which opera in this country was as rare as the Crown Jewels. Travelling companies had done no more than lift half-way a curtain. None of Beecham's company, or few of them, had already achieved fame. We did not go to Quay Street to hear and witness a Callas, a Sutherland, a Björling, a Schwarzkopf, a Tebaldi. We went to hear and see opera; we went to hear Mozart, Wagner, Moussorgsky, Verdi. Each and every evening was a voyage of discovery. These audiences at Quay Street were eager to enter the imaginative world of the different composers presented. They were not all of them musically unsophisticated. In those days, music was not produced in mass for the millions. Beecham's opera audiences in Manchester and the Hallé Concert audiences were made up of much the same people. And the ranks of both of them contained many of Manchester's rich Jews who had established shipping houses and lived in the city for decades. They knew their opera, having heard great performances in Germany and Austria. The rare point of these Beecham opera seasons is that the main attraction of them was not individual virtuosity or "publicity prepared" personal glamour; the intention and end frequently achieved by Sir Thomas was ensemble and relevance of style to the work in hand. Inevitably mishaps occurred to an enterprise so bold and so manifold. Scenery would go astray. The pressure at rehearsals was terrific, and there were not too many of them. A Beecham chorus was known to rehearse in the train bringing the company from London to Manchester. At a Covent Garden Beecham season, during a performance of "Das Rheingold," after the change from the Rhine to Valhalla, as Wotan and Fricka engaged themselves in argument, a man walked across the backcloth of Valhalla carrying a ladder on his right shoulder; a stage-hand had taken the wrong turning. A white-moustached gentleman, in white tie, sitting next to me in the stalls, grasped my knee and said, " Sir, did you see that? " My affirmative seemed to relieve him, for he released my knee and breathed: " Thank God! "

In Manchester we enjoyed an advantage over London in the productions brought to us from Covent Garden. We heard the finished performance. " Boris Godounov " was sumptuous, with a setting by Benois—pagan temptation to the senses in a Nonconformist citadel. Boris was sung and acted by Auguste Bouillez, a Belgian. Beecham couldn't engage Chaliapin, for his Manchester seasons; Bouillez was the next best exponent of Boris alive at this time of the century. He was Christoff's double in the part. Neither could measure himself with Chaliapin in the part, without diminishing vocal and physical stature. " If I were asked to look back over the years," Sir Thomas has written, " and to say in which of them I considered the British people were to be seen at their best, I should choose the period of 1915-1916." Certainly I have not known on the Continent or in the Southern hemisphere an audience for music as honest in its reactions, and as ready to collaborate with artists in humble grateful sensitive reception, as the audiences which went to the Hallé Concerts and to the Beecham Opera in this period of Beecham's retrospective choice. A London musical or opera audience of 1961 is sophisticated enough, God knows; sophisticated enough on matters of voice production and instrumental correctitude. I heard the other year two youths discussing a piano recital of Artur Rubinstein in the recital's interval: "I prefer his records," said one suède-shoed connoisseur, "there are no wrong notes."

Beecham kindled fires of warm solace to our nation as it lived through a war bloody beyond any massed human slaughter known before or since. Were we escapists? —to use the idiotic term of to-day. Men in khaki sat side by side with listeners who had lost sons in the mud and horror of France; they all sat under this Beecham enchantment. It was Sir Thomas's finest hour.

And what good came of it last? Sir Thomas was drawn into the entanglement of the Covent Garden Estate and Chancery. With the ending of the war a slump set in, reducing pockets everywhere. The British National Opera tried hard to reap from the Beecham sowing; but, as a fact, Beecham had reaped all that he sowed. Moreover, he had set up standards of opera production so high that the public would not support the very excellent second-best

playing the piano

broadcasting

of the British National Opera Company, despite their many memorable performances, notably one of Debussy's "Pelléas et Mélisande," conducted by Eugène Goossens; and another of "Der Rosenkavalier," brilliantly conducted by young John Barbirolli. And from the British National Opera Company emerged Malcolm Sargent. A lost cause nevertheless; the B.N.O.C. expired in 1929. As Hamilton Harty said, "British opera is dying—slowly but surely dying—of T.B."

For nearly a decade Sir Thomas receded in my particular musical scene. Harty, now in charge of the Hallé Orchestra, would allow no visiting conductor. So the wheel of my book has swung round to the day in Salzburg when he bought my first "White Lady."

From Salzburg he went direct to the Leeds Festival, and conducted with the panache and daring of a man in the full vintage of his life. He was now fifty-two years old. Without a score he explored and held together Delius's "A Mass of Life." At the time, the performance quite bowled me over; the sheer beauty of tone, vocal and instrumental, intoxicated me. Sir Thomas, two years earlier, had conducted the same work at the Delius Festival he organised in the Queen's Hall, London, in the presence of the blind, paralysed composer, who sat in a bath-chair looking like Lazarus. To organise this Delius celebration so that not a detail should go wrong, Beecham went specially to Delius's home at Grez-sur-Loing. He stayed all of one

Sunday discussing scores. He stayed on for dinner and when it had reached the liqueur and cigar stage, Delius sadly told Sir Thomas that, though the evening was young at nine o'clock, the last train would depart from Grez-sur-Loing at nine-thirty; and owing to his health and tendency to nocturnal fits of terrible spasms, laryngeal and of the body, he couldn't put Sir Thomas up. "That is quite all right," said Sir Thomas, "please open another bottle of your exquisite claret, Frederick. I have a taxi waiting." All day the taxi had waited, the driver fortifying himself at an adjacent inn—at Sir Thomas's expense.

Sir Thomas's conducting at the Leeds Festival of "A Mass of Life" and the superb singing and playing affected me deeply. In the "Manchester Guardian" I described the work as the most beautiful of all Masses for ravishment of tone. Later this seemed to me excessive praise, and I almost apologised to Sir Thomas that I had been guilty of uncritical exaggeration. "But, my dear fellow," he said, "you didn't exaggerate. You merely pointed out an obvious truth. No other 'Mass' approaches the vocal sensuousness of Delius. In fact such loveliness of sound, orchestral and vocal, would have gone contrary to a 'Mass' by Bach or Beethoven, even if either of these composers could possibly have written likewise—which, of course, was not within the scope of any musical style of their period. Delius's 'Mass' is pagan and therefore suited by an uninhibited sensuousness of tone. Where in all vocal music is there such richness of blended parts as in the 'Nocturne' of the Delius 'Mass' or in the hymn to 'Midday'?"

Now began our close friendship as untroubled as a noon day of calm cloudless sky in summer, interrupted now and again by sudden hurricanes, thunder and lightning and bolts of brimstone contumely aimed at me. The more he assailed me, privately and in public, the more fond of him I became. After the " Rosenkavalier " row about " cuts," we didn't meet for a year or thereabouts. Our reunion happened as we found ourselves in the same ascending hotel lift. " It is time," he said, " that we buried the hatchet—but let us carefully mark the place."

The incorrigible playboy in him broke out during the Covent Garden season of 1935. A new Italian soprano was announced, a discovery of Sir Thomas, her name Lisa Perli. She sang Mimi in " La Bohème," and the critics mainly praised her sky high. But she wasn't Italian at all. Her name was Dora Labette, who had been before the British public some years. Sir Thomas arranged the hoax to demonstrate how far a foreign name would go in England and English music towards spell-binding audiences and critics into unrestrained admiration. The secret of Signorina Perli's identity was closely guarded. When Sir Thomas took me into his confidence he threatened me with all manner of punishment if I " breathed a word." He would " unhair me, spifflicate me, break every bone in my body, belabour me with bludgeon and bastinado." Miss Labette went around heavily veiled, and arriving at the Covent Garden stage door would say, " I no speek-a Inglish."

But at the first rehearsal of " La Bohème," at the point where Mimi first comes into the scene, a player of the double-bass, peering on tiptoe and catching a view of the stage, involuntarily declaimed, " Blow me down if it isn't Dora ! " And in a voice of awful menace, Sir Thomas roared, " Signorina Perli, if you don't mind . . ." Dora Labette was, and still is, one of the most warm-natured laughing women I have ever known. Also she sang sweetly, whether as Dora or Lisa. I brought down on my head all of Sir Thomas's wrath when, in 1938, I took " Lisa " to task after a performance at Covent Garden. She was cast for Marguerite in Gounod's " Faust." " In this performance," I wrote, " even Lisa Perli, whose Marguerite came within the realms of sensibility—even she seemed frequently cold and inanimate. In the ' Jewel ' song she went through the contents of the casket as though going through the week's laundry." And very much like him, during our Australian journey, to come soon after this phrase had roused his ire, he often, in Dora's presence, chortled with glee as he quoted to her—" went through the casket as though going through the week's laundry . . . ha, ha, ha ! " He would choke; his laughter, once it was set going, was unbridled. As a rule, however, he apparently shared the opinion of Lord Chesterfield, who denounced audible laughter as ill-bred and illiberal—" true wit, or sense, never yet made anybody laugh; they are above it."

The imps of mischief and levity, permanently housed in Sir Thomas's mind, no doubt were responsible for the opinion, shared by many musicians, that he lacked seriousness at bottom. "Pagliacco," Toscanini called him (among other epithets). It is beyond doubt, too, that Sir Thomas did not conduct, at his best, the profoundest sorts of music: the B minor Mass, the "Missa Solemnis," the Ninth Symphony, "Tristan und Isolde," to name a few names. Yet none of his contemporary conductors equalled the simple dignity and sublimity of Sir Thomas's "Zauberflöte," or his treatment of the Papageno and Papagena parts. Mozart, indeed, was the only composer he would never conduct with deliberate naughtiness. Much as he admired Handel, he would tinker with his scores, respecting neither Handel's natural diction nor his period's essential style. At Covent Garden in the mid 1930s, he gave us an interpretation of "Siegfried" that for two acts was a musical delight, finished in detail, and balanced to a glowing serenity. Then, in the third act, he went berserk. Melchior and Leider panted and toiled after him in vain. The stylish beginning ended in irresponsible riot. Again I chastised him in print—why had he so wilfully let down a superb first and second act? Next day, for once in a blue moon not angry at a bad notice, he explained: "You critics are inhumane. I chanced to look at my watch, laid on the desk before me, and we were still not half-way through Act III —it was getting on for eleven o'clock. In the audience were many poor souls who had to go home to remote habitations such as Putney, Streatham and Swiss Cottage. And the public houses would close at eleven, and my orchestra, slaving away since six o'clock, were thirsty. So I just let Wagner rip!"

At a rehearsal of " La Bohème " Sir Thomas stopped the orchestra to speak to the tenor as he lay on the bed as Mimi was dying. " I can't hear you. Sing up! " And the tenor, I fancy it was the mellifluous Heddle Nash, replied with some spirit. " How do you expect me to sing my best in this position, Sir Thomas? " To which Sir Thomas replied, " In that position, my dear fellow, I have performed some of my greatest achievements." A rehearsal directed by him has been described by Yehudi Menuhin as a friendly gathering, a " picnic." Perhaps we should have likened Sir Thomas not to Falstaff but to Sir Toby Belch. " Dost thou think, Herr Furtwängler and/or Signor Toscanini, because thou art virtuous, there shall be no more cakes and ale? " I argued with him over Huberman who filled concert halls in Berlin and Vienna but had hard work to attract audiences in London. Huberman was a penetrating artist despite that his tone many times wounded the ear, sharp and inclined to depart from pitch. He used a steel E string, and could make all the others sound like it. " You should engage him to play the Brahms concerto with you, Sir Thomas." " I agree," Sir Thomas replied, with the familiar suave purr in his voice, " I agree that Huberman is a very fine artist, penetrating, as you say. But as a violinist, he has a certain defect." " And what is it? " I asked. " He can't play the violin," said Sir Thomas.

At last he engaged Huberman to play the Brahms concerto, and the performance was one to cherish. Greatness of style and fineness of style were mingled; energy was concentrated into eloquent lines, each alive with the current of Huberman's temperament, each controlled by Sir Thomas's own musical instinct; the whole conception set against a warm and realised orchestral background. A definitive performance in the Queen's Hall. Sir Thomas was happy in obtaining an easeful blending of tone at the awkward beginning of the slow movement, where the harmonies in the wind instruments call for the most careful balance—and seldom receive it. The rounded delicacy of this introduction caused me almost to tremble that Huberman's tone, which could sting like a whip, would enter abruptly and tear the brown autumnal twilight texture. But his tone did not *enter*: it descended light as air. Then Huberman transformed the solo violin's ornamentation into free floating melody; we might have been deluded into thinking that he, and not the orchestra, was playing the adagio's self-subsistent song. He infused into the general mazefulness, which is Brahms's main and obvious contribution to the movement, a deeper note than is usually there. This was done by means of a firm grasp of the patterns or periods of ornament, and by a tone which, though thoroughly musical and expressive of shading didn't become sensuous, let alone sentimental. As a consequence, we felt a continuous strength and authority; this was the proper Brahms of the adagio.

Before the event Huberman had suffered some anxiety about Sir Thomas's conducting of the concerto at rehearsal. Huberman had a habit, during an orchestral tutti (while the soloist wasn't playing) of bending down and cleaning his instrument and plucking the strings. Beecham halted the rehearsing orchestra, turned round and looked hard at Huberman, and asked, "what are you doing down there, Herr Huberman?" After the concert, Huberman was, for him, animatedly joyful. His squint of eye got even more diagonal—and this is saying much. "Your Sir Thomas, is a Zauberer, a magician in Konzert—at rehearsal 'e loves his jokes!" And Sir Thomas?—what was his opinion of Huberman now that he had heard him in a great performance? "Very good—very good indeed. I was quite taken aback, quite astonished." Simply that and nothing more.

In the 1930s Sir Thomas ruled the roost at Covent Garden (and now and then it was a roost), with Lady Cunard beneficent behind the scenes. His Wagner season of 1935 was extraordinarily interesting; he conducted Lotte Lehmann, Melchior, Leider, Böckelmann and List. At least one of these artists complained that Sir Thomas's tempi were too quick for clear articulate vocal phrasing. He answered the charge by the old familiar statement that a metronome test would establish that his tempi were generally slower than Richter's. The tendency of German conductors of Wagner has usually been towards emphasis on harmonic change and fullness; such emphasis favoured a conception of "The Ring" which had implications of philosophy. Sir Thomas concentrated on the dramatic and picturesque parts of the score. I doubt if he often looked at Wagner's verbal text. In "The Ring" the orchestra was for Sir Thomas three parts of the cycle's substance and interest. Seldom has Wagner sounded as elegantly garbed of texture as in these "Ring" performances at Covent Garden in 1935. If we missed a deep fundamental tone and a consequent solemnity, we received in exchange a rare beauty of musical shapeliness. When I described in my paper a "Götterdämmerung" performance in which Sir Thomas certainly "reduced the stature of the work," he replied, "But such was my intention."

His detractors said that Sir Thomas was at his best conducting second-rate music. There's no denying that he could poise and polish second-rate music so that it took an unaccustomed appeal. Soon after the opening of London's Royal Festival Hall, Sir Thomas "put on" a lightweight programme for a Saturday night audience. Out of my affection for him I was present. In this "popular" programme the prominent work was Goldmark's symphony "Die ländliche Hochzeit" ("The Rustic Wedding"), which Richter occasionally conducted at a Hallé Concert in my early years. The loveliness of Sir Thomas's phrasing of Goldmark's delicately sentimental melodies in the "Garden" movement, and the warm yet gentle tone of the Royal Philharmonic Orchestra, were such that I shall try never to forget their ingratiating appeal. The symphony sounded a miniature masterpiece; the first movement (a set of variations—and does any other symphony begin with variations?) flowed beautifully and abundantly—"Why in God's name," many of us asked that Saturday night of necromancy in the Royal Festival Hall, "why isn't this symphony in the permanent orchestral repertory?" The answer, emphatic and quite demonstrably negative, was given us a short time afterwards, by another conductor.

The strange fact of my long experience of Sir Thomas's conducting is that his performances of minor, or not of the first-class composers, stay in the memory, but his treatment of the composers who reside on the mountain tops tends to slip the memory, unless it was downright bad. We can all recall at will Beecham performances of Delius, Bizet, Tchaikovsky, Puccini, Rimsky-Korsakov, and a host of this charming kin. Apart from his Mozart performances, his name will not, I guess, be immortally associated with the greatest composers. G. H. Lewes, writing on Edmund Kean, maintained that "the greatest artist is he who is greatest in the higher reaches of his art." By this test Sir Thomas must be placed below Toscanini, Klemperer, Furtwängler and Bruno Walter, each one of his contemporaries.

Haydn?—I had nearly forgotten that Sir Thomas was completely happy conducting Haydn; but here the surface of the style, related to Mozart's, he could comprehend at a glance. Sir Thomas performed with felicity the second symphony of Brahms, the fourth, sixth and eighth of Beethoven. Indeed with felicity! But on the whole he tended to reduce the stature, the form and the spaciousness of music of intellectual substance. Artur Schnabel even disliked Beecham's conducting of Mozart: "He makes Mozart into a dancing master."

Sir Thomas could find the wave-length of Berlioz

whose music appealed to his un-German ear, sense of rhythm, and also to his tremendous confidence in himself as an *accoucheur*. He was one of the first of our conductors to understand the irregular lengths of the Berlioz phrasing and metre. I have referred above to his treatment of the Berlioz "Requiem Mass." A performance of the "Symphonie Fantastique" by the Hallé Orchestra also counts among my lasting impressions. Sir Thomas could penetrate deeply enough the remotest parts of any score he really liked. Too frequently did the imp in him not like a score for reasons he couldn't rationalise. At a Leeds Festival he conducted a wonderfully musical "Eroica" symphony, ridding the music of mid-19th century weightiness and tonal gestures supposedly earth-and-heaven storming. On the other hand, his conducting of the Ninth symphony, at an Edinburgh Festival, was deliberately made to sound empty and loose of structure. "Beethoven was the first cause of the disruption of music's natural style and speech," he would argue. Self-contradiction criss-crossed in his electrical intelligence. He, the absolutist, lover of sounding air and patterns, all revolving round a point of rest, was the most satisfying conductor of his day at unfolding the "narrative" of Strauss's "Ein Heldenleben." During a rehearsal of "Ein Heldenleben" he asked the trumpeters to play the fanfare announcing the battle-section from a place immediately outside the platform. "A more dramatic effect is obtained if the audience don't see you at this point of the score." The trumpeters were climbing towards the exit, when Sir Thomas, with an expression of anxiety in voice and gesture, said: " You will come back, won't you?" It was his conducting of " Ein Heldenleben " which delighted Strauss when, in 1947, he came to London for the last time at the age of eighty-three. Sir Thomas arranged a Strauss concert for the old man at the Drury Lane Theatre. Strauss sat in a box, and after a brilliant performance by the solo violin of the Polonaise in the " Bourgeois Gentilhomme " suite, he applauded spontaneously and noisily, only to receive from Sir Thomas a very peremptory " shush " before he began the next movement. From the conductor's chair, at Covent Garden, Sir Thomas commanded a member of the Royal Family to " Shut up," during a performance of an opera overture. Give him a work after his heart and he was the wholly absorbed artist whenever in action with the baton; and if sometimes he was as much absorbed in his own artistry as in the composer's music, none of us was the worse for it.

He didn't pretend to have a universal range; he was fond of quoting Oscar Wilde to the effect that only the auctioneer is under an obligation to admire all schools of art. Yet his range was broad enough, extending from Boccherini to Sibelius. After all, there are many more minor than major composers. Sir Thomas might not have lifted us, except now and then, to the heights where the austere masters dwell (and sometimes repose); no other conductor has equalled him in a consistent dispensation of musical pleasure. What he lost on swings he more than recovered on the roundabouts. Tragedy contracts, like an obsession. The spirit of comedy made Sir Thomas expansive, so that he was able to win a response from many first-, second- or third-rate quarters. If his musical vision was not unrestricted —and no conductor has traversed the musical field in all directions—he could embrace more composers than was in the scope of any of his living colleagues. If he sometimes missed getting to the heart of Bach and Beethoven at their greatest, he knew the sound of their voices. If he failed to sustain intensity in "Tristan und Isolde," as Furtwängler sustained it, his interpretation of "Die Meistersinger" was truer to the opera's genial style than Furtwängler's or Toscanini's. And there was always up his sleeve the trump card of his Mozart. His repertoire of opera hasn't been equalled in numbers by any conductor, alive or dead. From Grètry to "Elektra," from Rossini to the "Otello" and "Falstaff" of Verdi, he found the main style, even if occasionally he a little diminished it. So with his orchestral repertoire: put before him Handel, Cherubini, Haydn, Mendelssohn, Schubert, Brahms, Tchaikovsky, Strauss, Delius, Sibelius— he understood the language of all of these, which is rather more than we can say of Toscanini, Furtwängler, Klemperer and others.

At a Hallé Concert in the old Free Trade Hall on an October night in the crowd were many young folk who were hearing great music perhaps for the first time, in the very place where I first heard great music during the Richter days. This Beecham Hallé Concert was the opening concert of a Hallé season; and the programme began with Richter's favourite "Die Meistersinger"—the overture. Sir Thomas, thirty years ago not as huge of bulk as Richter, charmed this music into a guise which might have deceived Richter altogether—*gemütlich* humour gave way to brilliant arrogance. Then, in the second symphony of the "Salomon" set, he attended as diligently to Haydn's coiffure as the Friseur in "Rosenkavalier" attends to the Marschallin. The phrases were petted, caressed; but there was no danger of effeminate effect, for the simple reason that no power on earth could hurt the masculinity of the Hallé (or of Haydn). At this same concert, Sir Thomas rode the whirlwind of Tchaikovsky's "Francesca da Rimini"—Dante in terms of Doré. His gestures, his sudden doublings-up, his sudden movement upwards, the ferocity of his left fist, the dartings and swishings of his baton, seemed to bring the hell-fire section of the work visually before us. Incidentally, he achieved the best square cut I had seen since Charles Macartney, the incomparable Australian batsman.

Other conductors aim at a fairly complete representation of an orchestral score, with the inner parts identified. Sir Thomas insisted on definition of the "key" melodies. He believed that if a conductor applies himself to the outlines, to the songfulness and to the basic rhythm, details of texture could be trusted to fall into place. And if he should lighten the harmonic web, appearing to fillet a symphony—take it off the bone, as the waiters say—his audiences, goggle-eared, were content with the translated music dancing before them, content that Sir Thomas was content to be himself.

How was it that after one rehearsal or two he would stamp his style on an orchestra which had a different conception from his own of the functioning of great music, an orchestra like the Hallé, nurtured and nourished on solid German sustenance? It was his humour to pretend that rehearsals should be taken easily, taken as read. "At a rehearsal," he said, "I let the orchestra play as they like. At the concert I make them play as *I* like." He didn't expound the "meaning" of music to his players at a rehearsal, after the manner of many soulful Continental conductors—thus: "I want a fierce staccato!—here we all sigh—ghostly—now, gentlemen, crescendo—the passion is spending—we sink, we sink . . ." No; I have known Sir Thomas enter the Free Trade Hall in Manchester to rehearse the Hallé on a bitter foggy morning. Temperature very low, the auditorium opaque. "Good morning, gentlemen," he greeted the instrumentalists; "Now, where are we? Ah, yes, Delius—'In a summer garden,' very suitable for this occasion. Does anybody wish to play this piece? Or shall we begin with Strauss's 'Till Eulenspiegel'? Not in to-night's programme? Very strange; I could have sworn that it was. 'Don Quixote'?—ah, I knew we had to play something by Strauss . . . Now, gentlemen, I'm sure I needn't tell you anything about 'Don Quixote.' I certainly don't intend this morning, or any other morning of the year, to emulate the conductor who was an hour telling an orchestra that a 'tone-poem' of his own composition depicted the invasion of this island of ours by barbaric tribes, who swarmed in long boats over the wintry sea. This conductor, a native of England, gentlemen, became very eloquent as he described a passage in the tone-poem which was supposed to suggest slaughter, bloody relentless scenes of ravage, desolation, and doom. And after he had finished, his first violin asked, 'Excuse me, Professor, did all that happen before the war?'" With subsidence of the laughter he began again: "Our next piece, gentlemen, is, I think, the 'Enigma' variations of Elgar. A pretty piece . . . a thousand pities that Elgar was so much lured into composing oratorios and symphonies . . . 'Gerontius?' I hear someone ask. Well, gentlemen, 'Gerontius' is the kind of work Mendelssohn might have composed, supposing he could have visited Bayreuth and listened to 'Parsifal' . . ." He turned over the pages of the score of the "Enigma" variations . . . "I won't ask you to play this morning the first five numbers. Let us begin with the viola variation. And when we reach 'Nimrod' we must be very careful. I have been chastised by the critics because, so they say, I conduct the movement too quickly. So, gentlemen, if I seem to you to linger overmuch, you just go ahead and take no notice of me . . . Then, in the twelfth variation, I'd like the 'cello to languish . . . it's a lovely tune . . . *salon* music, gentlemen, *salon* music. So now—number six . . . I really can't ask you to play numbers one and two three times within forty-eight

listening to himself

at rehearsal

hours . . . Dear old Elgar—he is furious with me for drastically cutting his A flat symphony—it's a very long work, the musical equivalent of the Towers of St. Pancras Station—neo-Gothic, you know . . ."

"Let us begin. Would you kindly give us your A?" (this to the oboist, who having been out late the night before, produces from his instrument a frail wobble of a tune). Sir Thomas then said, "Gentlemen, take your choice."

At rehearsal he usually let the orchestra play a piece straight through before going into details; himself he sat back following the music with his beat. After this preliminary canter he would make his comment. "Er—Mr. So-and-So, I am entirely with you in your obvious reluctance to rehearse on a morning as chilly and dismal as this—but please do try to keep in touch with us from time to time."

One day there was a face strange to him among the woodwind. "Er Mr.——?"

"Ball," came the reply.

"I beg your pardon?"

"Ball, Sir Thomas."

"Ball? Ah—*Ball*. Very singular."

Now and then he would leave the conductor's desk and go to the back of the hall to listen, while his first violin conducted. And many times I have been amazed at the immediate difference in tone and phrasing while he was not at his desk. An extraordinary point about his conducting was that he seldom repeated at the concert, "on the night," the performance we had heard at the rehearsal. The concert performance had a fresh, spontaneous flight of melody and elasticity of rhythm. A performance by Toscanini, to take one example of another conductor's methods, was much the same as the performance concluded at the last rehearsal. More than any other conductor Sir Thomas understood the point of view of English orchestral players, even if he would brook no argument.

" We always play it this way," his first violin might say.

" Really," Sir Thomas would reply, affability itself, adding, " Very well—play it that way for Sir Malcolm and Sir Adrian. This morning you will all play it my way. And please, gentlemen, follow this beard, not that one " —his finger first indicating his chin, then his first violin. This particular rehearsal was with the B.B.C. Orchestra.

During the Delius Festival in London in 1929 " A Mass of Life " was being rehearsed. An argument began concerning the notation for the wind in a certain passage. (Sir Thomas was rehearsing from memory.) He turned to Delius, who sat all sprawled in his chair like a rag doll. " Frederick," he called, " I am engaged in some slight controversy with my first flute. Perhaps you'd be so good as to settle the issue? " Delius answered, " It sounded all right to me." Whereat Sir Thomas opened the full orchestral score lying on his desk, whipped over a handful of pages, scrutinised one of them and turned again to Delius, saying —" As I thought—A natural. Frederick, I wish you would take the trouble to memorise your own music! " He had been right about the disputed passage.

In his book on the composer, Sir Thomas has written of Delius's music, " It is imperative to maintain a tight control over the motion of the melodic line; otherwise there may be created an unpleasant sense of lassitude or shapelessness." Many times in conversation with me he expressed the opinion that nearly every conductor of Delius made the mistake of thinking that the first thing that had to be attended to in Delius was his " wash " of harmony. " It is all wrong to treat Delius as essentially a composer of vague shifting textures. He was essentially a melodist. Your fraternity "—(meaning the music critics)—" have a positive genius for saying the wrong thing. They insist that Delius possessed only a slight melodic gift. The fact is there is perhaps too much melody in Delius. When I conduct his music I turn to the wind to control a melody, and behind my back, so to say, the 'cellos begin another melody. I am, in fact *surrounded* by melody ! " We tend to forget that it was Sir Thomas who, out of his love for " A Mass of Life " brought Fischer-Dieskau to England for the first time, to sing the Zarathustra part in this work. Moreover, Fischer-Dieskau sang Delius from memory—a wonderful tribute to Delius; for he had gone to the arduous labour of learning by heart music he is unlikely to be called on to sing ever again in all his life. " A Mass of Life " is nowadays not performed on the Continent, and not more than once in every English blue moon. The fate of Delius's music in the future, as far as performances go, is in a precarious balance, now that Sir Thomas is no longer here to conduct it. I asked him only a month or so before his death, if there wasn't some serious structural defect in Delius's music, proved by the fact that only he, Sir Thomas, could give it shape and continuous vitality. "The defect is not in Delius. As I have frequently told you, it is the barbarous age we live in that is incapable of understanding such music, an age in which no new work could possibly appeal if it revealed evidence of breeding, delicacy, a sense of regret and a craving for beauty. Any work of art that at once attracts and satisfies our present age is sure—in fact, it is *obliged*—to be, brutal or frustrated and entirely lacking simplicity and modesty."

He swerved not a moment from a belief that "A Mass of Life" is a unique masterpiece. In his book on Delius he writes: "In 1923 we find Heseltine comparing 'A Mass of Life' favourably with the great Mass in B minor of Bach, and the first natural reaction to this claim is 'Why not?' Twenty years later Professor Arthur Hutchings finds the comparison absurd; and the equally reasonable comment on that is 'Why?' It is a pity that the learned professor does not condescend to advance any argument in support of his opinion, which is hardly respectful to his readers."

It was confidence in himself of the strong kind indicated in the view expressed above which was perhaps the secret of his influence over orchestras—plus, of course, knowledge of the score. An amateur, maybe—but an amateur of genius! As far as baton technique goes, it might almost be said that he had little of it. Many orchestra players have told me he had none. I have seen him get his baton entangled in his coat tails. Famous opera singers have assured me that they received scant help from him on the stage; he concentrated on the orchestra. How, then, did he conduct the most powerful and thoroughly controlled "Elektra" of our time? Was it personal magnetism? These same famous singers have agreed that while he conducted an opera he relied much on the prompter (" 'Tis the voice of the prompter, I heard you complain; he has prompted you once, he will prompt you again" was one of his choice sayings). His eyes were immensely persuasive, the whole man of him dominated people and situations. He knew, baton technique or none, how at once to find and maintain tempo. We might think this tempo was too quick or too slow but, once established, he managed it with consistency to his overall conception of the music's onward course.

I have referred earlier in these pages to a performance of the "Eroica" symphony conducted by Beecham—at the Leeds Music Festival of 1931. I have by chance found the notice I wrote of this performance in the "Manchester Guardian," and I take the liberty of quoting from it, *à propos* the question we are now asking—How did he get his effects—with a dubious baton technique?

"I have seldom heard Beethoven sound so stylish a composer as he sounded this afternoon. Beecham obtained from the orchestra the strength and that grotesque energy which is Beethoven's unparalleled characteristic, but he expressed these things without letting us feel for a moment that Beethoven mistook his medium by working in the materials of music instead of the materials of sculpture. The interpretation was an announcement of the power of rhythmical sensibility. Perhaps there is nothing much in the art of conducting beyond an acute understanding of rhythm—at least in the conducting of a symphony. The great virtue is to keep the music in vital and relevant motion towards the appointed end. Beecham's pulse seldom weakens. But how does he contrive to make instrumentalists play miles above their normal selves? I have not the ghost of an idea . . ."

Nearly thirty years after the writing of that notice I find the same question pretty unanswerable in words of rational content.

The persuasiveness he exercised on orchestras he exercised in his private life. In short, he was born to regard everybody and all things as somehow submissive to him. He knew how to order people about; more important still, he knew how to order people about in such a way that they were pleased to be ordered about—by Sir Thomas! "Have you ever been at a loss for a word?" I asked him, "ever been unable to cope with a situation at any time of your life?"

He thought about it for a few moments. "Yes," he replied. "Once . . . I was rehearsing 'Tristan.' And that glorious singer Walter Widdop was Tristan. I was obliged to pull him up—no small act of courage, for Walter, an intrepid Yorkshireman, feared nobody. 'Walter,' I said, 'you are singing divinely. But, really, you must carry yourself with more dignity, more pride of carriage. Don't you know who Tristan is supposed to be?' And Walter answered, ''E's only a sailor, isn't 'e?' I was rendered speechless, entirely speechless."

For the best part of his career he conducted from memory; his first and brilliant performance of "Elektra" was done without score. In his last years he took to using scores in public. No doubt he found them engrossing, holding the attention from first page to last. "The score at a performance," he argued, "gets in my way, stands between me and the orchestra, short-circuiting personal rays of influence. And anyhow, it is the instrumentalists who make the sounds—out of which I make the music." He edited scores minutely, bar by bar, "hairpins" everywhere. Without scruple he would rearrange a work if he felt that it needed to be adapted to the circumstances in which it was about to be played. Dynamics, loudness and softness, should be controlled and calculated according to the hall's size and acoustics. "You know, my dear fellow, not all the classic composers really understood orchestration so extensively that they could always make their music 'sit' happily on every instrument. Then, again, many of them composed in a period in which certain instruments had a different character, a different pitch, than is possessed by instruments to-day bearing the same names. I also take care to consider the receptive power of the audience. I don't agree with Mahler's axiom that 'if a slow movement is not going down well with the audience, play it a little slower.' Oh, dear no! If I sense any tedium or lack of interest in the audience, I quicken the music and make it louder and louder. I never conduct above an audience's head. It is an impertinence to do so. The audience has paid to be pleased—and great music invites many different treatments. There is, as well, the not-unimportant question as to whether the music is beginning to bore me. If it is—very well! I get it over as quickly as possible." He could absent himself most refreshingly from cant. But he would be down like a ton of hard bricks should any stranger tell him that he had deliberately conducted too quickly and too loudly.

He loved to present himself as a spirit of denial, a debunker of naïve enthusiasms. I have heard him prick a bubble of appreciation blown up in a breath of adulation of himself by some starry-eyed Beecham addict. There was the case of the large Englishman who burst into the artists' room of the Mozarteum at Salzburg after Sir Thomas had conducted the performance of the second symphony of Brahms played by the Vienna Philharmonic Orchestra. Nobody present in the artists' room knew who this large Englishman was—he really did burst in and began to rave —" Sir Thomas, what conducting, what tempi, what élan! And the Vienna Phil., what an orchestra, what a tone, what strings, what ensemble, what style!" Sir Thomas looked up from his chair at the large Englishman. "Have you ever heard the Bournemouth Orchestra?" he asked. The large Englishman collapsed, a pricked balloon. He left the artists' room and we saw no more of him.

As I say, with any music he loved he was devoted—and a marvel of patient attention to details. He was never flippant when he was directing a recording of his orchestra and his conducting. It is a boon to us that some of his finest music-making is " preserved " by the gramophone. Notably his incomparable interpretation of " Zauberflöte," with a connoisseur cast—Lemnitz, Hüsch, Roswänge, Berger and Strienz. No other conductor has achieved Beecham's balance and blend of solemnity and felicity in this opera, wisdom and prattling innocence. He found the right pace and quantity of tone for the " March of the Priests " and his shading of the choral ending of Sarastro's " O Isis " brought tears to the eyes and brings them to mine to this day whenever I play the records. Nobody has equalled his ethereal touch in the Trio of the Three Boys—the A major Allegretto. Nobody has equalled his timing of the dialogue recitative of Tamino and the Priest. This incalculable Beecham—Toscanini's " Pagliacco "!—conducted " Zauberflöte " with an unparalleled mingling of objectivity and personal sensibility, so that the opera came to us fresh as creation, solemnity gently passing like a cloud over sunlit heavens, so that at least to one listener the wonderful lines were recalled of the Angels in the " Prologue " of Goethe's " Faust "

Und alle deine hohen Werke
Sind herrlich wie am ersten Tag

Sir Thomas did not often allow emotion to come into his voice when he talked to you. But one evening he spoke of " Zauberflöte " and as he referred to the sublime downward curve of " Tamino mein " he was obliged several times to clear his throat. Then, covering himself, he said " so simple—and the labour pains suffered by the moderns ! "

It was probably the mischievous imp in him which kept him, as a conductor, out of the " world-class " occupied by Toscanini, Klemperer, Furtwängler and Bruno Walter, that same irrepressible imp which contributed so richly and endearingly to the joy of life. At a rehearsal of the " Messiah " he pulled up the Australian soprano, Thea Phillips—" My dear, what is the matter with you? You are not singing the right notes. And I imagined that every English-speaking child babbled the ' Messiah ' music in the cradle." Miss Phillips, trembling in every nerve and bone, stammered, " B-b-but it'll be all right at the performance t-to-morrow, S-Sir Thomas. I've been working hard on the score for months and t-t-taking it to bed with me every night." " Ah," said Sir Thomas, " then I'm sure we shall have an immaculate conception."

The same imp spoke here that offered " Lollipops " to his public and prompted him to ask the tuba player, who had gurgled wrongly with a bowel rumble the " shake " towards the end of the " Meistersinger " overture, if he would now " Please pull the chain."

Music couldn't contain him. He might have made a name as a Q.C., as a financier, as a critic of books, a critic with prejudice, defying augury. Or he might have controlled a huge business, reducing every tycoon to perplexity, as they wondered what he would do next. I cannot imagine a Toscanini, Klemperer, Bruno Walter or a Furtwängler putting music out of their lives for years, while they were engrossed in the winding-up of an Estate. Music was not for Sir Thomas the only way of life; he took it in his stride. His quicksilver mind was perpetually adventuring. He should, of course, have created a Glyndebourne years in advance of John Christie's achievement. But he found working in harness distasteful. "*L'état c'est moi!*" We should, as we think of him now as a conductor, remember that he had to organise the medium, the paraphernalia and the whole arena, for his activities. A Toscanini, a Bruno Walter could at the outset of a career find at hand an opera house, a technique and tradition developed over many years, encouraged and sustained by princely or State patronage. Beecham, as we have seen, began from scratch, removed the dust from British musical institutions, opened windows to let in a cleansing air. He led us out of the German captivity; he mediterraneanised our music. At one time of Sir Thomas's career certain of his critics argued that he was unable to create a school or an influence of lasting use tangible enough to be handed down. His activities in opera were brilliant but evanescent. There is no evidence to-day at Covent Garden that he was once director there. He reorganised the London Symphony Orchestra—and left it. He formed the London Philharmonic Orchestra—and left it. When he was gathering together the London Philharmonic I chanced to be present one day to hear him discussing its probable membership with Lady Cunard.

"I have found the best trumpeter in this or any other country—a man from Blackpool," he said. "Blackpool?" asked Lady Cunard pertly, "but only the other day you told me he came from Wolverhampton." "And, my dear," replied Sir Thomas, "he did originally hail from Wolverhampton. But the climate and the atmosphere there affected his lungs, so he went to Blackpool to get the benefit of the fresh air." His last and happily abiding instrumental "creation" was the Royal Philharmonic Orchestra, which to the end of his days he maintained was "the finest extant." Its future, we may rest assured, is safe in the care of Lady Shirley Beecham.

But he was himself his most finished, unique and most thoroughly rehearsed production. He enlarged his personality continually. Not always, as we have seen, was he the Sir Thomas who, in his last years, became an admired and loved institution. When he was dapper middle-aged Mr. Beecham, he seemed in the eyes (and ears) of many people a personification *in excelsis* of the Bounder. In time he presented himself as Sir Thomas, G.O.M. In the fullness of his years he was best savoured in private with a few friends, the light winking on the wine glasses' brims. The smoke of his cigar, a sort of materialisation of his fancifulness, visible shapes of his wit, curled on the intimate air of the elegant room in which we sat, lost to measurable time. In his company now, the troubles of the world would disperse. In these moments of Sir Thomas's ease, nobody would have dreamed of speaking of any trouble of the world, or even of the most grievous personal sorrow, for fear of seeming trivial. His presence was pungent. His affability and his superb suggestions of sureness of self temporarily insulated him from care, responsibility and all mundane worry—and, moreover, insulated those sitting with him. His every word and movement was a virtuoso performance of self-expression, self-realisation.

I came to love him, his poses and his high disdain, his courteousness and his rudeness, his intolerance and his generosity—all these variable traits mingled in the shot-silk of his temperament.

He was one of those casually masterful men, flavourers of life, whom we cannot imagine overtaken and put down by death, that most repetitive of bores. At my last meeting with him, a Sunday night not long ago in his suite, he quite calmly planned his next decade or so, casting a very wide and loose net. He would go here and there; he would conduct 18th-century music of a very select order; he would buy a house in France "—the only civilised place left on the face of the earth"; he would conduct very few operas—"no singers to-day, my dear fellow. They all require microphones." He would collect precious plate and antique furniture. Life, he was beginning to realise, begins at seventy—"in fact, the first seventy years are the worst."

Cosmopolitan and Lancastrian, a man in whom wit

was enriched by humour, in whom knowledge was changed to culture by sensibility; a complex man of uninhibited mind and temperament, with the gentle cynicism acquired during the passing of years in a world's centre; bland, enigmatical, impulsive, selective—and sometimes capricious, the swift changes of the chameleon . . . Sir Thomas, or in good Lancashire vernacular, " Tommy."

On his seventieth birthday he was entertained to lunch by a great host of his admirers. Telegrams and cables from distinguished persons arrived from all parts of the world. To reverberating applause the chairman read them out, one after another. " Congratulations," " Greetings " —from Strauss, Stravinsky, Hindemith, and so on; then, finally, from Sibelius. And as the cheering died down, Sir Thomas looked up to the chairman from his place at the table and asked, with a slightly pained expression on his face, " Nothing from Mozart? "

Now he lies still and anonymous in Woking cemetery. Woking? Why not Westminster Abbey?

THE END